ARCHITECTURAL DESIGN

EDITORIAL OFFICES:
42 LEINSTER GARDENS, LONDON W2 3AN
TEL: 0171-402 2141 FAX: 0171-723 9540

EDITOR: Maggie Toy
EDITORIAL TEAM: Cristina Fontoura,
Stephen Watt, Iona Baird
ART EDITOR: Andrea Bettella
CHIEF DESIGNER: Mario Bettella
DESIGNERS: Sonia Brooks-Fisher,
Alistair Probert

CONSULTANTS: Catherine Cooke, Terry
Farrell, Kenneth Frampton, Charles Jencks,
Heinrich Klotz, Leon Krier, Robert Maxwell,
Demetri Porphyrios, Kenneth Powell, Colin
Rowe, Derek Walker

SUBSCRIPTION OFFICES:
UK: ACADEMY GROUP LTD
42 LEINSTER GARDENS
LONDON W2 3AN
TEL: 0171-402 2141 FAX: 0171-723 9540

USA AND CANADA: VCH PUBLISHERS NEW
YORK INC, SUITE 907, 220 EAST 23RD STREET
NEW YORK, NY 10010-4606
TEL: (212) 683 8333 FAX: (212) 779 8890

ALL OTHER COUNTRIES:
VCH VERLAGSGESELLSCHAFT MBH
BOSCHSTRASSE 12, POSTFACH 101161
69451 WEINHEIM
FEDERAL REPUBLIC OF GERMANY
TEL: +49 6201 606 148 FAX: +49 6201 606 184

Architectural Design is published six times per year (Jan/Feb; Mar/
Apr; May/Jun; Jul/Aug; Sept/Oct; and Nov/Dec). Subscription rates for
1996 (incl p&p): Annual subscription price: UK only £68.00, World DM
195, USA $142.00 for regular subscribers. Student rate: UK only
£50.00, World DM 156, USA $105.00 incl postage and handling
charges. Individual issues: £16.95/DM 42.50 (plus £2.40/DM 6 for
p&p, per issue ordered), US $28.95 (incl p&p).
For the USA and Canada, Architectural Design is distributed by
VCH Publishers New York Inc, Suite 907, 220 East 23rd Street
New York, NY 10010-4606; Tel: (212) 683 8333, Fax: (212)
779 8890. Application to mail at second-class postage rates is
pending at New York, NY. POSTMASTER. Send address changes
to Architectural Design, VCH Publishers New York Inc, Suite
907, 220 East 23rd Street, New York, NY 10010-4606. Printed
in Italy. Origination by Media 2000, London.
All prices are subject to change without notice. [ISSN: 0003-8504]

CONTENTS

Battle McCarthy and
Eric Kuhne & Associates,
daylighting analysis for
bluewater retail development

Brian Clarke, Haus der
Energie, Kassel, Germany

Ortner and Ortner, Europä
Design Depot, Klagenfurt,
Germany

GUY BATTLE AND CHRISTOPHER McCARTHY

MULTI-SOURCE SYNTHESIS
Towards the Light

He saw; but blasted with excess of light
Closed his eyes in endless night.
Thomas Gray, *Elegy in a Churchyard*

An increase in the intensity of light is not what
we need. It is already much too strong, and can
no longer be tolerated by our eyes. Tempered
light is what we need. Not 'More light' but 'More
coloured light!' must be the call . . . Colour-
tempered light settles the nerves, and it is used
by neurologists as an element in the cures at
their sanatoria . . .
Paul Scheerbart, *Glasarchitektur*, 1914

The science of light and the technology of its manipulation is highly advanced. We can create lasers to destroy missiles in space or make tiny incisions in human tissue, and control the emission of single protons, yet our understanding of the human response to light is simplistic and poorly researched. Conventional lighting design aims only to achieve sufficient illumination at the minimum cost, ignoring its influence on mood, perception and comfort.

Lighting design or analysis is too often an afterthought to the design of a building, when it could be the generator of form. Light creates space and emotion, and should be one of the principal media of the architect engineer. The future of architecture is sculpting in light.

Electromagnetic spectrum
The electromagnetic spectrum ranges from gamma and X-rays at the short end of the spectrum to radio waves and Extremely Low Frequency waves (ELF) used for submarine communication. In the centre is the range of wavelengths that our eyes are sensitive to, the visible spectrum; from 3.8×10^{-7}m (blue) to 7.6×10^{-7}m (red). Beyond blue is ultraviolet which can damage the skin, whilst beyond red is infra-red, or radiant heat.

Electromagnetic radiation consists of fluctuations in the electric and magnetic fields, which take place at right angles to each other. Like ripples in a pond, disturbances in the electromagnetic field spread out from the source. All electromagnetic waves move at the same speed (299,792 kms) but travel more slowly through different materials (glass 198,223kms).

The human eye is our passport to this world. The retina contains 6.5 million cones, responsive to colour and intensity, and 125 million rods which are more sensitive but perceive only the quality of light not its hue. There are more cones at the centre of the field of vision and more rods at its periphery, explaining why during periods of low illumination objects are brighter in the peripherals than the centre.

We can perceive a huge range of light levels. The rods begin operating at a surface luminance of 0.001cd/m² (candelas per metre squared), at 3cd/m² the cones start operating and at 1,000cd/m² the pupil closes down to its minimum. To put these into perspective the full moon emits 2,500cd/m², the filament of a standard incandescent light 7,000,000cd/m² and the surface of the sun 1,650,000,000cd/m².

Human response
In Sweden, at the beginning of every dark winter, more and more people start to make a daily trip to the local medical centre, to sit for 30 minutes dressed entirely in white in a bright room flooded with 10,000 lux of daylight-spectrum light. These individuals are sufferers from Seasonally Affective Disorder (SAD), a recently recognised phenomenon. Without light therapy, SAD sufferers become depressed, tired and irritable when the winter sets in and daylight hours drop below a certain level. SAD is thought to be linked to the pituitary gland – the 'third eye' which controls key body functions including sleep and the perception of time – and is an interesting example of how light influences the way we feel and perceive.

Human responses to light vary with climate, culture and the individual. For most people, red light is 'warm' and blue light is 'cold'. However people from Southern Europe will be more comfortable on a hot day in a dark or shuttered room, whilst people from Northern Europe would rather be in a warming bright light.

Researchers have discovered that fluctuating illumination in the workplace throughout the day influences productivity; greater production can be achieved by gradually raising the intensity of lighting at certain times. Similarly, at the centre of deep plan buildings lighting is maintained at higher levels than near to the windows, to compensate for the lack of perceived daylight.

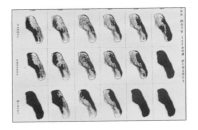

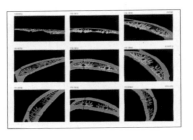

FROM ABOVE: Sequential photographs of lunar eclipse; solar analysis, Holy Island, with Andrew Wright; solar analysis, L'Ile Seguin, with Richard Rogers Partnership

II

Lighting design

Lighting is conventionally designed to provide a constant specified light level at the working plane, with the spacing and layout of luminaires being determined through simple calculations. More recently the reduction of energy use, through the maximisation of daylighting, has become a priority as lighting accounts for up to 20 per cent of the electrical demands for an average building. This approach involves plan depths of between 12 and 15 metres, carefully designed windows and shading systems and the use of 'intelligent' computer controls linked to dimmer switches and external lighting sensors, but can reduce lighting energy use by 60 per cent or more.

There is a variety of new and existing tools which allow the design team greater freedom to explore the uses of lighting within their buildings, but despite this the majority of designers still rely on more traditional methods. The analysis of crude cardboard models under an artificial sky – even though they reproduce a mere 10,000 lux, the 'Standard CIE overcast sky' – and the heliodon, which provides a simple mechanical method to observe sunlight penetration and shadows, remain the most popular tools used during the early stages of the design process. However, much more powerful computer-based applications are being evolved which enable dynamic three-dimensional and generative modelling.

The software programme RADIANCE can be used to provide accurate predictions of daylight levels – plotted as points or contours within space and photorealistic renderings of interiors and exteriors – for different times of the day and year, as well as varying weather conditions. Animation can be used to watch the sun's movement through a space over a year, or the penetration of shadows into external spaces. Alternatively the viewer can assume the viewpoint of the sun and fly over their building, generating a direct appreciation of the effectiveness of shading devices or solar reflectors.

Working on a variety of projects, Battle McCarthy is applying combinations of computer tools enabling the architects to sculpt in light. For the Tate Gallery, Bankside (with Alsop and Störmer) a mixture of simple and intuitive analysis was used to develop a series of 'paintings' exploring the impact that internal variations in light and temperature would have on the visitor. The firm proposed that the illumination of each new gallery, projecting through the redundant box of the power station, could respond to its proximity to the river, external wind speed or even the colour balance of paintings and sculptures.

For the National Glass Centre (with Gollifer Associates), light transmitting materials and associated technologies were used to manipulate lighting; including photochromic, thermo-chromic and electrochromic materials, holographic glazing and electroluminescent displays. The building will perform its function as an exhibition centre for glass as much in its materials and form as in the displays which occupy its spaces.

Generative modelling

The next step will be to use generative models. If a designer's primary interest is the manipulation of human experience through light, these programmes will enable him to generate hundreds of different forms, in response to a three-dimensional model of illumination and colour; as these proposals are modified so the shape of the building will alter. The building becomes a 'back projection' with emitted photons defining a building on their way to rejoining the sun. This generation of computers will allow the designer to visualise and walk through light as solid objects or mist . . . where the visible becomes invisible. The light flooding through an opening becomes a swelling form to be manipulated.

Even now the lighting designers for 'raves' are pushing back traditional barriers, utilising light and music to create space and heighten the senses. Hopefully in the future architects will learn from this, creating three-dimensional 'lightforms'; specifying colours and intensities based on an understanding of mood.

We have only just begun to ask the questions that lead to a true understanding of light, and to progress any further designers must begin to explore human interaction with different colours and intensities; its influence on mood, and our perception of space, temperature, time and comfort. Lighting design briefs must extend beyond the prosaic minimum specification, inviting architects to sculpt light as they do space.

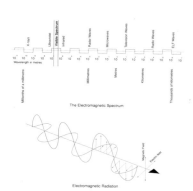

FROM ABOVE: Visible light is a small part of the total electromagnetic spectrum, whose wavelength varies from millionths of millimetres (X-rays) to thousands of kilometres; heliodon used to model solar penetration; analysis of drawing office; computer analysis of light output from one source

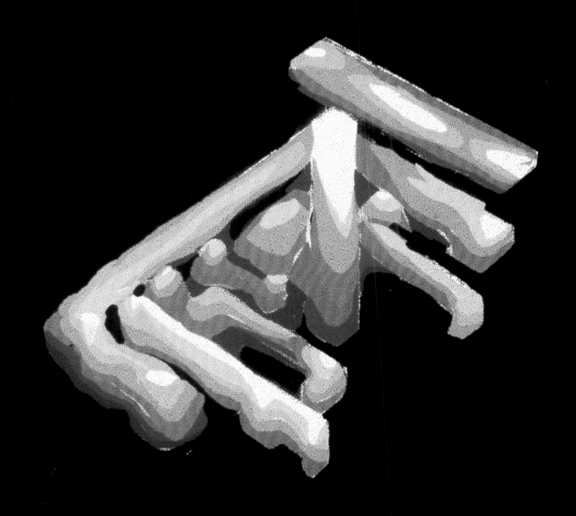

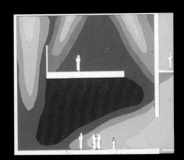

Competition entry for the new Tate at
Bankside, with Alsop & Störmer. Based on
simple and intuitive analysis, a series of
drawings was produced to explore the idea
of sculpting in light, so that the experience
of the visitor is to wander through a constantly changing set of light and temperature
experiences, responding to the location of
the gallery and the type of works shown.
ABOVE: Drawing of daylight levels in the
overall form; FROM L TO R: Model of
proposal; lighting studies

OPPOSITE ABOVE: Daylight analysis;
OPPOSITE BELOW: Daylighting analysis for
Bluewater retail development, with Eric Kuhne
& Associates, carried out with Integrated
Environmental Solutions using RADIANCE.
The objective has been to create a shopping
street with a similar variation in environmental
conditions to an external street, but without
the drawbacks of weather and cold.
Daylighting is one of the environmental
variables that the design team has to balance
against temperature, air movement, and
energy use to create a successful design.
For example, the desire for a daylit space
creates the requirement for 60 per cent of
the roof to be glazed, but this creates a
higher cooling requirement and makes it
more difficult to naturally ventilate the space.
In this case it is more energy efficient to
reduce the amount of glazing and rely on
electric light than to increase the cooling load.

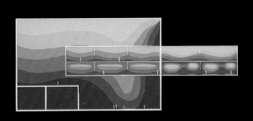

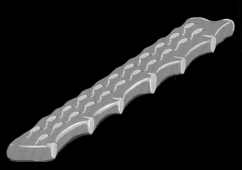

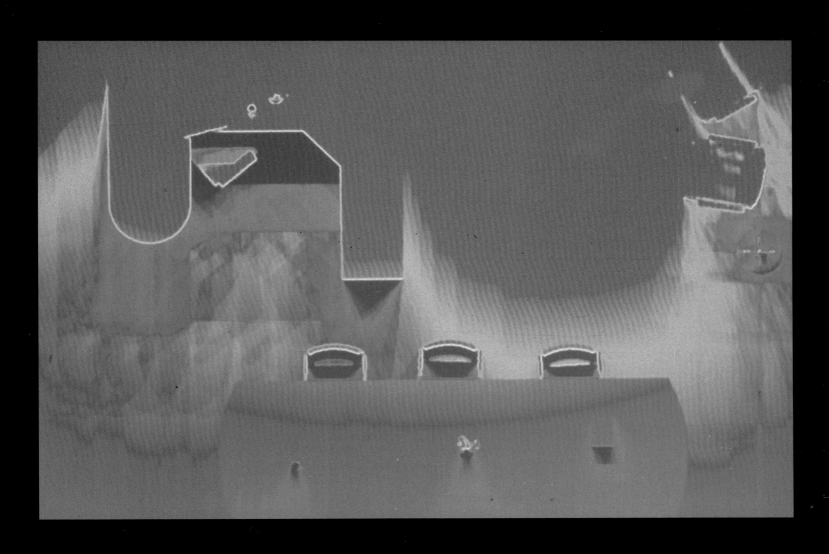

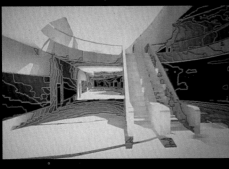 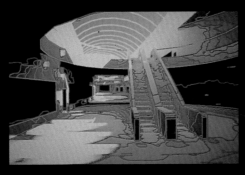 

v

JOHN PICKERING
CYBERSPACE AND THE ARCHITECTURE OF POWER

The technique of reproduction detaches the reproduced object from the domain of tradition.

This is Walter Benjamin, writing in 1936 on the effects of the mechanical reproduction of cultural icons and the material basis of aesthetics. Even if there has not been the revolution that he predicted, what he sensed about technology has helped to create an arena of revolutionary cultural change. This is the almost real world of electronic communication and entertainment, the icon of contemporary culture known as cyberspace. What Benjamin foresaw was the significance of the simulacrum, the multiple and mobile virtual thing which stands for a fixed and singular reality. While 'virtual' formerly meant 'almost', its recent usage, as in 'virtual reality', now stands for 'real-seeming', the world of cyberspace and the simulacrum.

Almost 60 years after Benjamin's prophetic intimation of virtual reality, the technology of simulacra is re-shaping our cultural arena. It is becoming possible to act in virtual space as if the meanings of reality had been imported into it. Mobile virtual meaning is central to what Lyotard has called the libidinal economy of post-industrial culture, where fluid sign value has come to dominate the more solidified values of use and exchange. Not only reproduction but also production itself are becoming virtual. Cultural icons are now forming, reforming and miscegenating in a domain of electronic magic, conjuring up a menagerie of androgynous cyborgs with human voices which stride, roll and flap through spaceports, street-fights and medieval castles.

These chimeric inhabitants and simulated vistas may make cyberspace seem to appear little more than an arena for games. However, what is being played out there is more significant than that. The hybridisation of myth and technology reflects something central to Postmodern culture as it winds into the future, turning on itself in a cross-linked helix of quotation and ironic juxtaposition. As in game playing so in cultural appreciation, self-conscious eclecticism is the rule. These games are assembled both from real events, like the Gulf War and from cultural clichés like the gunfight, and in a similar way, the built environment is composed from this embellishment, those proportions, that vista. In games or architectural appreciation, quotation and double-coding is ubiquitous, the common currency of stylistic pluralism and self-awareness.

The sensitive tip of the helix is in the media, whence there gushes a 'flood of information' about the 'flood of information' that electronic technology has unleashed. Cyberspace is presented not only as a place but also as a movement; a frontier with a populist surge showing where culture is going. As satellite dishes sprout from roof tops and the cable burrows into suburban front rooms, the coming electronic wonderland is celebrated and clichés about the sudden transformations that the Internet will bring are already worn smooth.

Things move fast in cyberspace and as academics ponder over its significance, it appears that the academy itself is about to be engulfed. A recent edition of *The Times Higher Education Supplement* (THES) suggested that the Internet would cause another Gutenberg revolution in academic publishing 'overnight'. The same issue carried pictures of children amidst an array of screens, pressing glowing yellow buttons and grasping joysticks. The screens were windows into spaces where things could be done like shopping or exploring. No keyboards and very few words were in view, indeed, the children did not look old enough to read. Close to these pictures were details of WebSpace, an Internet browsing tool which, working beyond the linearity of texts or the two-dimensionality of images, allows travellers to ' . . . rotate, walk through and spin renderings of architecture . . . '

Cyberspace has architectural interest to the extent that it is increasingly able to display real space. Science fiction used to be about aliens and intergalactic travel, now it is about exploring the cultural space where human beings will renegotiate their identity with technological life forms and is rich with Apocalyptic visions of a culture dominated by artificial intelligence. These visions are images of the 'space behind the screen', as it was called by William Gibson, credited as the author who invented the term cyberspace. Here a 'highway' provides access to multiple-user domains. In these zones you can explore a world of rooms, spaces, doors and passages and interact with acquaintances, human or otherwise.

Researching this article, I investigated one of these world's called Lambdamoo and inquired about whether there was a map. I was told that there was one, but I have yet to find it. Unfortunately, the only way for me to interact within this domain is through words, which limits the region's spatial qualities. Even so, when talking about domains like Lambdamoo, it seems reasonable to use spatially-descriptive language. With more powerful equipment, utilising images, sounds, analogue controls and tactile feedback, users will experience a more natural interface and actually perceive the zone in terms of real space.

This is why cyberspace has architectural interest. Domains, and their structures, inevitably express meanings through their design, situation and use. A library is not merely a sign that books are to be found there but is also a symbol of value and authority. However, the structures of cyberspace hold information in new and powerful ways which exhibit a new sort of empowerment. What people encounter as they use cyberspace is not just the information that flickers across screens, but an icon for something much more than its use value; a potent sign of the powers of the medium. Unlike books the images on screen do more than represent information, they are interactive and if engaged, through user-interface, they access another screen connecting the operator to new domains and services.

It is this aspect of cyberspace which has a far more fundamental cultural significance, described by Baudrillard as the 'ecstasy of communication'. Electronic information and simulation is more mobile and flexible than it has ever been, reflecting the transition from an economy based on exchange value to one based on sign value, the state of post-industrial culture. With this shift has come the empowerment of the cognitariat. As architecture expresses the values of those with the power to shape the environment, it will reflect this as it encounters cyberspace. When the economic base was primarily material goods, structures were designed that were permanent and powerful enough to produce, house and to symbolise them. This became the solid masonry of 19th-century cities; factories, warehouses and civic buildings located in tight knit groups since their business depended on the material exchange. Together, these structures were not only functional but also broadcast messages of substance, *gravitas* and worth.

Society's economic basis has now shifted towards information services, and so the messages broadcast have shifted to mirror this. Post-industrial architects are conductors for a lighter but more mobile charge, concerning speed, fluidity and transformation. The material structures reflecting this culture, whose sensitive tip is now to be found in cyberspace, are exemplified in the communications industry. The large buildings that used to house the infrastructure of the telephone network now stand virtually empty, as the obsolete human operators and electromechanical equipment required vastly greater space than the computer-based systems that now do the job. Centralised urban locations are no longer a prerequisite for information based industries as illustrated by MacCormac, Jamieson & Pritchard's Cable and Wireless college, rippling gently in a greenfield site.

A building is a real workplace and while cyberspace is partly a virtual playground, it is also part of the nervous system of Post-modern culture. In fact, the cliché that cyberspace is a real place that people could visit, like a building or a country, can be treated seriously to some extent. There is a space, of sorts, with unique properties and potentials, and structures are being created in it that people can use and explore. It is, in a practical way, architecturally rich because radically new actions and structures are possible. The rhetoric of cyberspace is about empowerment and the meanings here are about mobility, access and power. You can surf the Internet, boldly go where you will, be what you want to be, do exciting transformative things, connect to the whole world and participate in the global cyber-democracy.

However, the reality is nothing like this as many of the users are just as likely to be computer nerds playing introverted computer games. What the great majority of people who enter cyberspace will be doing for quite a while yet, is just sitting at terminals, virtually motionless, with their eyes focused on a screen a few inches away. Also as most users are young white males in overdeveloped countries, using machines that cost more than lifetime earnings in the developing world, there is no global empowerment here. Given the current situation, more people are set to be disempowered than are empowered by cyberspace, so to hail it as the arena of global democracy is darkly ironic.

The falsity of cyberspace rhetoric is not only known, but is also consciously inflated. If Baudrillard is right that images of desire can become reality more rapidly than ever before, this means that reality can be talked into existence in a new and powerful way. It is because today's media gush is tomorrow's database and next month's product that there is something important going on. Even if most cyberbabble turns out to be mere Post-modern whimsy something important may happen in trying to make it reality. Take for example the overblown rhetoric of artificial intelligence in the 1970s when it was confidently predicted that computers were going to talk, think and have responsibilities and rights. They never did, but from trying to fulfil these inflated dreams enormously important things have been achieved. Computers do not use natural language, but 80 per cent of the translation in the European Commission is done by programs, not people. Neither do they think, but they still assist people who have real problems to solve. They do not have responsibilities or rights, but they do control situations with real consequences and so cannot be switched off.

Likewise, although the wilder reaches of cyberspace will stay fictional, important things will happen because explorers will try to get there. Virtual space will, eventually, become an arena for real action and the helix will leave behind it a trace of structures that have enough in common with real ones to be of architectural interest. However, despite the rhetoric of 'overnight' transformation, this process will be a matter of *bricollage* not breakthrough. No single aspect of information technology is going to open a magic gateway into an already-formed world of cybernetic structures. Admittedly, there are confident predictions for tools of enormous power, but the majority will fail or prove to be too specialised. Instead, accumulating tools and practices will gradually bring cyberspace into being. A number of these are already in place and others are appearing at an increasing rate; some of which will become incorporated into the practice of architecture. The glow below the horizon hints that the empire of information technocracy will be alight with glittering wonders.

In the mundane present, electronic equipment and practices are already found in architectural work, but they are generally used as labour saving devices. Eventually they will come to mean more than this. Again, consider artificial intelligence as an analogy. Computer programmes were expected to replace human decision makers. They did not, but what did emerge were decision support systems without which contemporary human decision makers would be unable to work at the rate they do. Indirectly, electronic intelligence has become incorporated into human practice and in doing so has changed fundamentally. Architectural practice will undergo a similar evolution since it has a particular character that fits well with what the tools and practices of cyberspace can offer. These are to do with visualisation, transformation and three-dimensional modelling. Buildings, environments and arenas for action can be created in virtual space and then entered in order that their layout and their

workings can be investigated.

As an example, consider designing compact turbines. Here wires, ducts and conduits have to be put near one another even though they carry things that cannot be mixed, like electricity, fuel and hot gasses. Too near, and there is danger, too far and the objective of compact design is compromised. This layout problem is addressed by systems that display a working drawing as a virtual space into which designers may enter at whatever scale required, say a few inches or so. Thus shrunk, they may walk around the prototype, much as a tourist would walk round a cathedral, carrying out alterations through perceptual-motor control. Once things are satisfactory, the designer returns to actual size, the design updated.

Systems with this sort of power are going to become increasingly affordable, permitting walk-through inspection and hands on re-design in real-time. These data-structures will be the working environment for surveying, estimating and designing modifications, with on site work being reserved for later stages of the contract. There may also be cross-fertilisation from other disciplines; for example, the rapid prototyping techniques now used in production engineering may be applied effectively to architecture if the transfer proves to be fundamentally a matter of re-scaling.

Thus, the impact of cyberspace on architecture will be piecemeal and come from different directions. It is not the pronouncements of cultural theorists that will bring cyberspace from virtual to actual reality, but the development of affordable working tools and the practices that go with them. These techniques will not only have to do with design, but with how this information is distributed and used, and this is where architectural practice may enter cyberspace in a fundamentally different way. Information and communication technology involves the rapid transfer and reproduction of any data structure, whilst architecture involves representations of space. If these representations, be they plans, drawings, texts or virtual prototypes, are created with electronic tools they will be able to migrate and to be worked on collectively far more extensively and rapidly than at present. Ways of displaying, storing and distributing architectural work, initially for commercial reasons will then become a more mobile resource, with clear implications on education in architecture, art and design, and the history of the built environment.

This process will participate in the generation of cyberspace itself. Many interesting designs are never built, but when designs appear in cyberspace, the boundary between the built and the not built is renegotiated. With time, the designs for what was actually built will

migrate and mingle with those that were not, transmitting the special cultural impulse that architecture bears in a new and powerful way. It will create places where designers, students, clients and tourists may do what they please, browse, look, interact, copy, modify and participate in the collective work. What will become manifest is the material trace of the present talk about cyberspace.

Of course, it did not require the advent of information technology for there to be spatially-aware descriptions about concepts which have no actual three-dimensional form. Space is implicit in how we describe our lives. We speak of 'getting into' a new 'area' when what we really mean is that we are thinking about investigating a new topic. Thus the characteristics of cyberspace can be treated with caution, as things that are not inherently three-dimensional have always attracted spatial metaphors.

However, what is intriguing about the impact of cyberspace on architectural practice is that the matters in hand are genuinely spatial to begin with, and these sensitivities may lead to a more realistic use of the medium making it more productive. Architecture is about creating the meanings and values of the built environment and with displaying them to clients. This requires a special type of creativity which is deployed in a hierarchy of media, from initial sketches, through working drawings, to the specification of materials and fixings. This is the skilled transformation of an artistic impulse into its material expression. The forces that are bringing cyberspace into being could benefit enormously from these skills.

These forces are not, of course, politically neutral, and the moguls of post-industrial capitalism have concentrated their attention on electronic technology for decades now. Bill Gates and Rupert Murdoch talk of the Internet as the ultimate production and distribution system. Just as the built environment of the industrial age expressed utility, production and accumulation, so cyberspace, the cutting edge of post-industrial culture, is rich with simulacra, mobility, reproduction and transmission. Simulacra are virtual, but not false. Hypertexts are real discourses, even if ink and paper may have disappeared. Databanks have information about real people and datastructures have information about real buildings. Despite their ethereal nature these structures are real enough; people may be talked to and the buildings visited. Power lies in access. Just who can and cannot interact in cyberspace, and what they may do there, is a sharp political and legal issue. The expression of power through virtual architecture is going to be as important as it is in the making of places like the Pentagon or the Kremlin.

Which returns us to Benjamin. Even though the technology of reproduction is still getting up to speed, the decoupling from tradition that he discerned is clear enough. Electronic architectural practice will move away from the aesthetic traditions of fine art and new sensitivities will develop. Benjamin felt that technology would democratise the material base of aesthetics by liberating the process of production from the control of an elite. However, it presently looks as if electronic means of reproduction will be as tightly controlled as were the means of production, despite cyberspace's portrayal as a democratic environment. In fact, as a means of production, reproduction and distribution, it is more subject to control. The result is a dark and ironic contrast between the image of cyberspace as the arena of social transformation and the rise of an elite cognitariat from the disempowered mass.

Cyberspace has architectural meaning that is as directly related to power as that of material buildings, and encounters with these will change how we perceive the built environment. This echoes what Benjamin felt mechanical simulacra would do to the visual arts. As reproduction modulates the aura of authenticity that surrounds works of art, so our sense of cultural habitation is bound to alter as structures are constructed in cyberspace. Their creation is a matter of architecture as well as programming. Some of the places being built will be very like real places, and virtual reality may even allow us to be in them to a degree that is real enough to be worth paying for. Of course, being there will still be the real thing. Visits to New York, with the noise and the pollution, will be vastly preferred to sitting in the living room with your head encased in a television set. However cyberspace travel to real places will soon be an affordable way of deciding where to go on holiday, or whether the new design for the city library is to our liking. How we then encounter these places will have been changed.

The glittering prize, though, is not to create the virtual travel brochure, but the palaces that express the imagination, free from the mundane constraints of service-duct provision and load-bearing calculations. Of course, cyberspace offers places to play, but these are dungeons that specify all too tightly what sort of games can be played in them; their design owing more to comics than the Bauhaus. Yet cyberspace may soon be more architecturally interesting as domains like Lambdamoo are starting to have human-scale functionality and real vistas where you can develop your own games to play. It is beginning to feel possible to be 'there' and to notice and respond to what it affords. The 'reality' of these domains will increase dramatically as it is created by individuals who design places that can be utilised in the way visitors desire, not in the way programmers intend.

Cyberspace games express a powerful play of signification; a cultural movement from the real towards the virtual. Despite the hype, its political and economic significance is in fact growing quickly, and the architectural values of this region will respond to the access and distribution of power, communication rights and the control of information and meaning. Even though cyberspace is an arena for games and fiction, important structures will remain when the media froth has blown away. There really is a 'space behind the screen', power is there and not just anyone can get to play with it.

As it participates in the cultural and political process it is not only the goods and services of the libidinal economy that will circulate. What will flow through it will be opinion surveys, subversive literature, directives of the United States of Europe, manifestos and votes. It is well to remember that Benjamin's prophetic essay ended with the insight that war marks the failure of society to incorporate technology. He also predicted that in a culture whose perception had been transformed by technology, simulacra would be used to beautify war and as Baudrillard pointed out this has already happened. The real Gulf War was virtually hidden by the most tightly controlled media campaign of modern times. The tragedy presented through video bites that had the dynamics and the aesthetics of a videogame. In a tightening cultural helix, as meaning becomes mobile and autonomous, virtual and real wargames are blending. Cyberspace play and work are both about the control of meaning and the expression of power, which is why its politics are the politics of architecture.

Virtual games are part of a real cultural and political impetus. To the extent that cyberspace comes to have a spatial character, and this impetus could be expressed through architectural practice. As it incorporates innovative electronic tools and practices, architecture will produce works that are detached from its present aesthetic traditions. What forms these will take is, however, still to emerge. Presently it seems that what is prefigured in cyberspace will participate, as Benjamin feared it would, in a celebration of destructive forces set loose when culture cannot contain the effects of technology. If architectural values and objectives can be expressed in cyberspace perhaps it will help to make it a more productive and civilised cultural arena.

j .pickering @ warwick.ac.uk

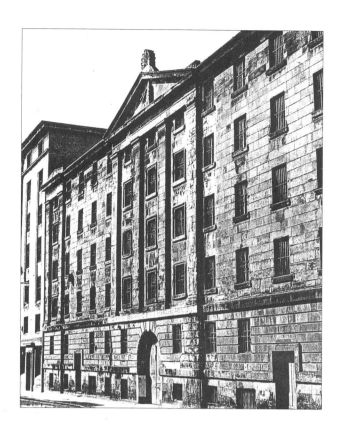

FROM ABOVE: A general merchandising warehouse, Glasgow, 1848; J & J Belcher, warehouse, London, 1885

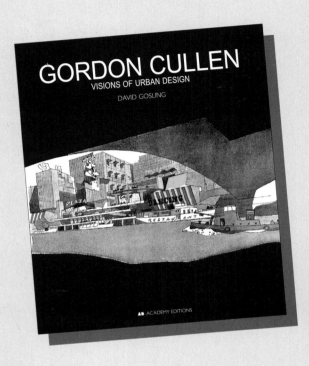

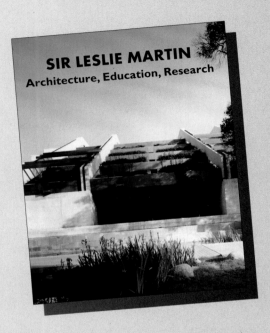

Gordon Cullen
Visions of Urban Design
David Gosling

Gordon Cullen was a key motivator and activist in the development of British theories of urban design in the post-war period. Illustrated with over 300 works selected from the thousands of drawings Gordon Cullen made during his lifetime, this anthology documents his influential career as an urban theorist, artist and illustrator from 1930 to 1990. The majority of his beautiful drawings has never been published before except in professional reports, and this book contains numerous drawings executed for the pleasure of observation as well as the product of his many consultancies. With the assistance of family and friends, the author charts Cullen's life and work and comment on his contribution to 20th-century urban design. His graphic techniques and their application and influence are examined as well as his attitude to the symbolism of objects in the environment.

Hardback 1 85490 435 3
305 x 252 mm, 256 pages
350 illustrations, mainly in colour
March 1996
£45.00 DM147.00 $70.00

Sir Leslie Martin
Architecture, Education, Research
Peter Carolin

The architect and urbanist Sir Leslie Martin, Professor of Architecture at Cambridge University, from 1956 to 1972, has been acclaimed as the leading architectural educator of the second half of this century in Britain. His strong belief in urban design, the organisation of low-rise medium density housing as opposed to tower blocks, and computer based research has placed him at the forefront of architectural education. A clear indicator of Martin's unique contribution to architectural education is that some 18 professors of architecture have emerged from his reign at Cambridge. Apart from his designs for the Royal Festival Hall in London and The Gallery of Modern Art in Lisbon, he has also designed a number of renowned academic or arts buildings at Oxford and Cambridge Universities and in Glasgow.

The book is edited by Professor Peter Carolin, a graduate of Sir Leslie Martin's school in the late 1960s, assisted by Martin's former colleague, Trevor Dannatt. It comprises numerous tributes together with detailed historical descriptions of his major works in Britain and Portugal.

Hardback 1 85490 441 8
279 x 217 mm, 208 pages
Over 200 illustrations, 50 in colour
March 1996
£35.00 DM98.00 $60.00

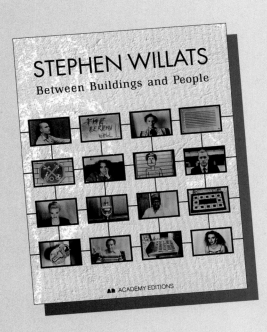

Stephen Willats
Between Buildings and People

For over 30 years Stephen Willats' work as an artist has involved an exploration of social relations and of contemporary life in urban society. The book centres around the interviews and photographic documentation made with people directly involved in their own environments, and explores the effects of the modernist built environment on people and how they express themselves creatively as individuals – for example the inhabitants of particular housing estates, workers in an office, and a variety of different working and living environments. Photographs are combined with statements where the viewer is guided by the artist bringing out a network of references and an infinite number of possible interpretations. Willats' deeply humanistic approach will be of great interest not only to artists and art students but also to architects, sociologists and cultural theorists.

Paperback 1 85490 436 1
279 x 217 mm, 144 pages
Over 100 b/w illustrations
April 1996
£17.95 DM50.00 $30.00

Russian Design
Traditions and Experiment
Yuri Nasarov and Alexander Lavrentivev

This book is the first comprehensive documentation of the entire history of design in the Soviet Union, and therefore of an era which has now ended. It examines the well-known design of the post-revolution years, which were characterised by Constructivism, as well as the design of tools and products for everyday use which were prevalent in the Stalinist period. The volume concludes with an analysis of the current trends which determine the contemporary debate in the former Soviet countries. Illustrated throughout, it presents a wealth of unknown material from a country which was closed to the West for many years and which shows surprising convergences with American design of the 1930s and 40s.

Hardback 1 85490 426 4
245 x 290mm, 160 pages
Illustrated throughout
1995
£32.50 DM80.00 $50.00

Further information can be obtained from
Academy Group Ltd, 42 Leinster Gardens, London W2 3AN, Tel: 0171 402 2141 Fax: 0171 723 9540, or from your local sales office:

National Book Network, 4720 Boston Way, Lanham, Maryland 20706, Tel: (301) 459 3366 Fax: (301) 459 2118;

VCH, Boschstrasse 12, Postfach 101161, 69451 Weinheim, Federal Republic of Germany, Tel: +49 6201 606 144 Fax: +49 6201 606 184;

reviews *books*

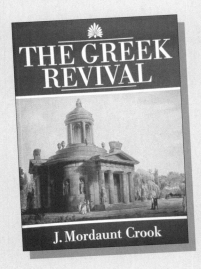

THE GREEK REVIVAL; NEO-CLASSICAL ATTITUDES IN BRITISH ARCHITECTURE 1760-1870 by J Mordaunt Crook, John Murray, 240pp, b/w ills, PB £19.99

First published in 1972, 44 years after Clark's appraisal of the Gothic Revival, Mordaunt Crook's text was the first to reassess the slightly earlier Greek Revival. The nadir of the English movement coincided with the staggered publication of what came to be regarded as its handbook: Stuart and Revett's *Antiquities of Athens* (1762, 1794, 1814, 1830) though by the end of this period, under the eclectic approach of men such as Barry and Cockerell, the style had become more generally Neo-Classical. Starting with Stuart's Doric landscape temple at Hagley (1758-59) Mordaunt Crook demonstrates how the movement sprang from 18th century Romanticism (both the Picturesque and the Sublime), the search for a purer way of life (and its concomitant retreat to historicism), and the new interest in Greek antiquities and archaeology nurtured by the Society of Dilettante. From this basis he shows how it developed from a 'fashionable conceit' into 'the very criteria for architectural distinction', the key year being 1804 when Wilkins defeated Wyatt in the competition for Downing College, Cambridge. For two decades hence the Greek Revival was to flourish, most notably and successfully in monumental public buildings, but also in domestic and ecclesiastical architecture. Like many of the 19th century critics who saw Neo-Classicism with its possibilities for abstraction as the key to a modern style, Mordaunt Crook's heroes are those who built 'not as the Greeks built, but as they would have built had they lived now'; men such as Soane, Cockerell, Barry and most of all, Alexander Greek Thompson. The black and white photographs of the book's pictorial section show as eloquently as Mordaunt Crook's arguments both the strengths and weaknesses of the Revival: the spatial and formal purity of Inwood's North London churches; the grandeur of Wilkins' and Smirke's museums; the inventive formal massing of Soane and Greek Thompson's wide variety of buildings; the stark austerity of Monck, Gell and Dobson's Belsay Hall; the ludicrous inappropriateness of James Knowle's Silverton Park. By 1829, when Cockerell and Playfair's National Monument stood unfinished on Edinburgh's Calton Hill, the Greek Revival was over, relinquished, concludes Mordaunt Crook, as too alien. The search for a true modern style would have to wait until the 20th century when Modernism would develop the structural rationalism implicit in the all the Revivalist styles which defined the 19th century.
R Bean

THE JAPAN GUIDE by Botond Bognor, Princeton Architectural Press, 336pp, b/w ills, PB

This guide aims to provide a brief, general introduction to the history, development and present course of contemporary Japanese architecture. It acquaints the reader with a vast number – 280 main entries and 360 other projects – of wide-ranging buildings and complexes which embody the highlights and unusual aspects of this architecture.

The 'handbook' feel is emphasised by its design, particularly that of the introduction and essay by Botond Bognor, in which he offers his criteria for inclusion and exclusion on the basis of limitations imposed by the country's architectural history. The further back you delve into the one-and-a-half centuries the book covers, the fewer buildings of note exist, either destroyed in the 1923 earthquake or during World War II. Japanese architecture developed apace with the incredible economic surge of the 1980s, and consequently, many smaller projects were demolished so that taller structures could rise efficiently among the dense urban areas. This period, Bognor explains, sees the development and 'maturation' of architects such as Tadao Ando, and of the so-called Shinohara school, including Ito and Hasegawa. On the whole, personal residences have been excluded for reasons of privacy, and the work of foreign architects is represented in the shape of Eisenman, Foster and Koolhaas, among others.

The primary function of this book – that of guide – is facilitated by over 30 maps of urban areas and major routes through Japan. Detailed information is given to enable easy on-site visits of all entries – exact addresses with both English and Japanese names, public transport and opening times, in conjunction with dates of public holidays, make this book a useful guide, but it also serves as a concise monograph of the subject.
S Parkin

STRUCTURAL GLASS by Peter Rice and Hugh Dutton, E & FN Spon imprint of Chapman & Hall, 144pp, colour and b/w ills, PB

This expanded second edition was completed shortly after Peter Rice's untimely death but he was, through many discussions with Hugh Dutton, a large contributor to the choice and inclusion of the projects to elaborate on the structural principles of suspended glazing as evolved for La Villette by the RFR team.

The book begins with a description of the properties of glass, examples of structural glass and an explanation of the decision to try to minimise the structure of the suspended glazing on the Serres (greenhouses) of the Cité des Sciences et de l'Industrie in Parc La Villette. The desired effect was to increase the transparency of the glass beyond that of the Willis Faber & Dumas office building, where the structural glass fins distort the transparent nature when viewed at an angle. The resultant cable truss structure and techniques of fixing glass 'allow structural elements to be eliminated from the glass plane'. The resolution of stresses, lateral bending and buckling and wind pressures in forming the principles of the horizontal cable trusses and the suspension system are explained in comprehensive detail and diagrammatic illustrations, including working drawings which show all the component parts.

The 15 projects illustrated in the postscript also exploit the technology which developed as a result of the work of RFR in the most dramatic use of glazing systems and glass. Innovation and creativity are apparent, as is an aesthetic simplicity which has developed from structural complexity and clearly integrates architectural objectives. Even in the use of glazing systems in Japan which are being designed to counteract typhoon conditions and seismic movements, the same principles

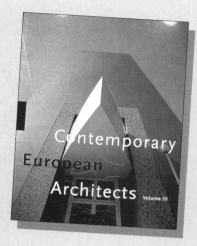

remain, with only minor modifications to the component parts.

This straightforward book is ideal for the study of the design innovations of Peter Rice and his team, illustrating as it does the aesthetic qualities and structural knowledge that the firm have employed in some of their most recent work. As acknowledged by Adrien Fainsilber, architect of the Serres at La Villette, 'Peter Rice's genius managed to persuade the industry "to think differently about the way to use glass" and to develop . . . industrial production'.
I Baird

CONTEMPORARY EUROPEAN ARCHITECTS VOL III by Philip Jodidio, Taschen, 176pp, 170 colour and b/w ills, PB £11.99

This book takes a selection of contemporary projects from all over Europe, some very familiar and some relatively obscure, which Jodidio discusses in the context of several current topics of interest. Among others, the debate includes new transportation and communication links, in relation to Grimshaw's Waterloo Terminal and Calatrava's Lyon-Satolas; France's Grand Projets, the Bibliothèque Nationale (not featured) and the Cité de la Musique by Christian de Potzamparc; and the development of many new cultural buildings in Europe such as the Groninger Museum by Alessandro Mendini, Coop Himmelb(l)au et al, and the Munster library by Bolles-Wilson.

Essentially, this book is not designed as an in-depth study of the individual works of architecture; it supplies 'tastes' of the work of some of the leading architects of Europe. The old favourites – Foster, Piano and Grimshaw – along with some of the newer generation are featured, but nevertheless there is a feeling of *déjà vu*. It is the kind of book bought by the general public and students because of its attractive presentation and price: as a full colour highly illustrated book it is good value for money. It is not however a serious critique of architecture or architectural style and does not provide enough material for a comprehensive understanding of any of the buildings featured.
I Baird

JAPANESE DESIGN; A SURVEY SINCE 1950 by Kathryn B Hiesinger and Felice Fischer, Philadelphia Museum of Art/Harry N Abrams Inc Publishers, pp236, colour and b/w ills, HB

This smart visual appraisal of Japanese design is the fruit of the Philadelphia Museum of Art's labours, published in conjunction with the exhibition of the same name and effectively serving as the catalogue of exhibits. Apparently the collection is the first of its kind in the world, and the book in itself provides a comprehensive overview worthy of adornment on any coffee-table.

However, there is more to marvel at than the over-zealous red symbolism and a mere flick through the pictures. A comprehensive introductory essay outlining the evolution of Japanese design is provided by the Philadelphia Museum of Art's Felice Fischer, Curator of Japanese Art, and Kathryn Hiesinger, Curator of European Decorative Arts. This is followed by a collection of ten short essays on topics as diverse as 'Design and Government' and 'Textiles and Kimonos', all of which give more detailed insight into individual areas of design. Designer Statements (for example Kazuo Kawasaki, Industrial Designer) and Company Histories (such as the Director of Nippon Design Centre and the General Manager of the Sony Corporation) ensue, providing a variety of contemporary perspectives, all from the actual designers involved.

The bulk of the book, 'the design survey' itself, comprises a glossy compendium of 250 products, furniture, textiles and graphics spanning intervals of ten years since 1950. This representative selection of a nation's post-war design output certainly reflects the nature of Japanese design: ancient culture and traditional craftsmanship combine with innovative dynamism; technological developments are eagerly embraced, invariably with humour; and the most mundane of objects are imbued with an aesthetic ethos whereby simplicity of form, colour and appearance generate the product's individual 'spirit'. Throughout, the high quality visuals are boldly presented, with concise product descriptions to accompany each image. Such organisation gives clear insight into the development of Japan's cutting-edge aesthetics over the past half decade.
LJ Ryan

LAKOV TCHERNIKHOV by Carlo Olmo and Alessandro De Magistrised (ed), Somogy Editions d'Art, (French language), 329pp, over 300 ills, 90 in colour, HB, 490FF

A lavish co-publication with Umberto Allemandi & Co, Turin, this book sets out to provide a full account of the legendary Lakov Tchernikhov (1889-1951), visionary artist, eclectic inventor, giant of Russian architecture of the 20th century. Making use of documents and reproductions from the archives preserved by his sons, a more complete picture of his work as an architect, designer, painter, writer, teacher than previously possible has been built up. Tchernikhov was one of the most prolific creative personalities of our century, his extraordinary output including monumental and grandiose architectural projects, futuristic architecture schemes worthy of the best science fiction movie, avant-garde graphic work, extensive typographic experiments, as well as exhaustive theoretical writings. He had a profound feeling for pre-Revolutionary Russian tradition as well as an Utopian vision of an industrial future but he shared the fate of many of his contemporaries in the Constructivist movement in that few of his projects were ever realised. His reputation has been revived in the last 15 years with a new generation of high tech and deconstructivist architects drawn to his dynamic and splintering forms which take Constructivist forms into a realm of architectural fantasy. Essays by his son Aleksei Tchernikhov, Anatoli Strigalev, Nicoletta Misler, Jean-Louis Cohen, Alessandro De Magistris present a diverse approach to the subject, attempting to show the unity of thought running through the seemingly disparate parts of his work. The book contains a large number of reproductions of the most exceptional quality which more than do justice to Tchernikhov's exuberant graphic skills and profound vision.
N Kearton

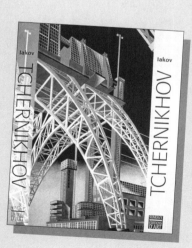

THE CARRIER
Nadim Karam

The restoration of the National Museum on the Place du Musée in Beirut is more than a reinvention of a city square, it represents a renewed hope of peace. In 1975, at the outbreak of civil war in Lebanon, the National Museum closed its doors and was placed on the front lines of the war. It was badly damaged and has become a war memorial: the damaged walls, smashed windows and hole in the 5th-century mosaic all witnesses to the events that have passed.

Nadim Karam designed a 15-metre-high metallic human form called the Carrier which appears to carry the roof of the National Museum building. The structure is steel and is covered with copper and bordered with strips of floral fabric. A dozen metal figures 2.5 metres high stand on top of the roof, and the Place du Musée houses an eagle and Roman columns. The Carrier took his place on 13 September 1995 and since then the square has become a meeting place for the citizens of Beirut, though the Museum has yet to open.

Photographs by Pascal Beaudenon

COLOUR IN ARCHITECTURE

VOETS ARCHITECTS, DELTA SCHOOL, DELFT, THE NETHERLANDS

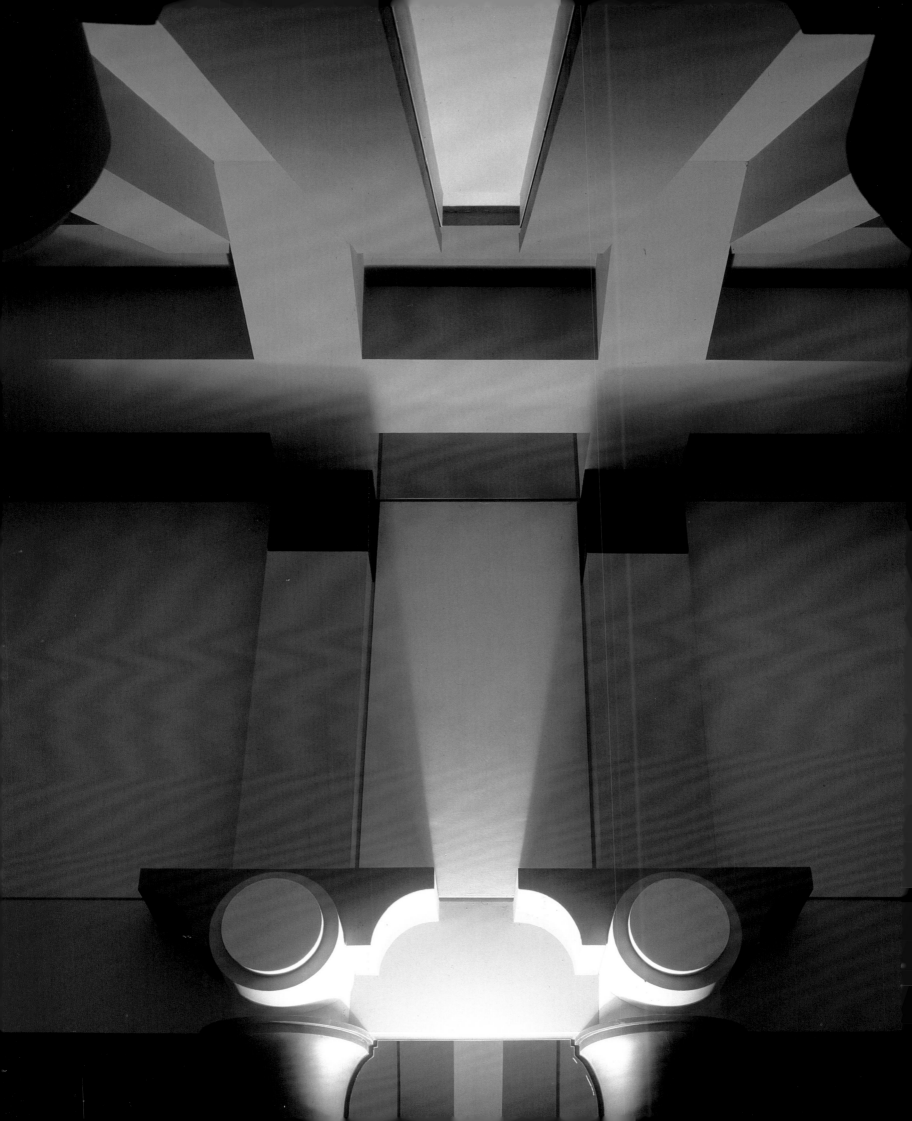

Architectural Design

COLOUR IN ARCHITECTURE

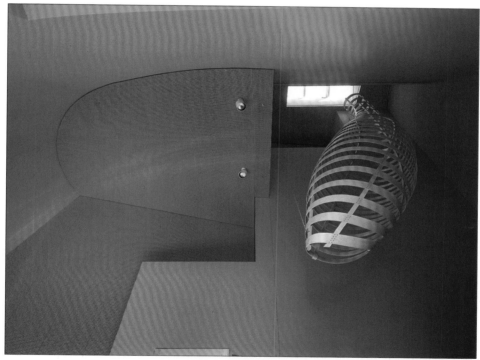

FRANK O GEHRY, VITRA INTERNATIONAL HEADQUARTERS, BASEL, SWITZERLAND;
OPPOSITE: JOHN OUTRAM ASSOCIATES, THE JUDGE INSTITUTE, CAMBRIDGE UNIVERSITY

ACADEMY EDITIONS · LONDON

Acknowledgements

All material is courtesy of the authors and architects unless otherwise stated. 'Colour in the City' is reprinted with the permission of Butterworth Heinemann, Oxford from *Urban Design: Ornament and Decoration*, by Cliff Moughtin, Taner Oc and Steven Tiesdell, published in 1995. 'Reading Form and Space: The Role of Colour in the City' is reprinted with permission of the Helsinki University of Art and Design from *Aspects of Colour*, by Harald Arnkil and Esa Hämälälnen (eds). We we also like to thank Michael Lancaster for permission to reproduce 'Seeing Colour' from his book, *Colourscapes*, published by Academy Group, 1996.

Front Cover: Antoine Predock, Museum of Science and Industry, Tampa, Florida
Inside Covers: Maurice Agis, Colourspace

Photographic Credits
All material is courtesy of the authors and architects unless otherwise stated.
Attempts have been made to locate sources of all photographs to obtain full reproduction rights, but in the very few cases where this process has failed to find the copyright holder, apologies are offered.
Joe C Aker *p26 (top left and top right)*; Diana Balmori sketches *pp28, 29 (top left)*; Paloma Brotons *pp96, inside cover*; Peter Cook *pp2, 72, 74, 75*; B Davis *p26 (bottom right), 29*; Thomas Dix *pp3, 84, 86, 87, 88, 89, 90, 91, 92, 93*; Chris Gascoigne *p82*; James Hedrich *pp38 (top right), 40-41, 42, 43*; Timothy Hursley *pp64, 66-67, 68, 69, 70, 71, cover*; Michael Lancaster *p23*; Lourdes Legorreta *pp5, 6, 32, 34, 35, 36, 38 (all except top right), 39*; Hugh MacConville *p10*; Jean-Marie Monthiers *pp44, 45, 46-47*; Tom Porter *p9*; T Sato *p26 (centre right)*; Bridget Smith *p94*; Ger van der Vlugt *p1, 48-49, 50, 52-53, 54, 55*

EDITOR: Maggie Toy
EDITORIAL TEAM: Cristina Fontoura, Stephen Watt, Iona Baird
ART EDITOR: Andrea Bettella   CHIEF DESIGNER: Mario Bettella   DESIGNER: Sonia Brooks-Fisher and Alastair Probert

CONSULTANTS: Catherine Cooke, Terry Farrell, Kenneth Frampton, Charles Jencks, Heinrich Klotz, Leon Krier, Robert Maxwell, Demetri Porphyrios, Kenneth Powell, Colin Rowe, Derek Walker

First published in Great Britain in 1996 by *Architectural Design* an imprint of
ACADEMY GROUP LTD, 42 LEINSTER GARDENS, LONDON W2 3AN
Member of the VCH Publishing Group
ISBN: 1 85490 256 3 (UK)

The Publishers and Editor do not hold themselves responsible for the opinions expressed by the writers of articles or letters in this magazine
Copyright of articles and illustrations may belong to individual writers or artists
Architectural Design Profile 120 is published as part of *Architectural Design* Vol 66 3-4/1996
Architectural Design Magazine is published six times a year and is available by subscription

Distributed to the trade in the United States of America by
NATIONAL BOOK NETWORK INC, 4720 BOSTON WAY, LANHAM, MARYLAND, 20706

Printed and bound in Italy

Contents

LEGORRETA ARCHITECTS, PLAZA REFORMA, MEXICO CITY

ARCHITECTURAL DESIGN PROFILE No 120

COLOUR IN ARCHITECTURE

EDITORIAL
Maggie Toy

Colour is an immensely evocative medium, possessing inherent powers to provoke immediate and marked reactions in the onlooker, and as such it has been developed as a language of symbol in both the natural and the man-made worlds. Its use in architecture is no exception, serving to dramatically affect perception of architectural space and form.

However, when incorporated into this discipline its highly subjective nature is also emphasised. Colour is one of the most unpredictable areas of architectural decoration: each individual's experiences differ and no amount of analysis can successfully foretell how people will respond to the same colour. Almost any generalisation that can be made about colour can be over turned in practice.

The use of colour is also connected with architectural fashion. In a previous issue of *Architectural Design* we focused on architects whose work tends to be termed 'minimal' – a development from the Modern Movement and International Style which abhorred the use of applied decoration. The colour scheme often associated with this type of design is based on variations of white which allow the colours and light in the surrounding environment to reflect into the space: thus the design lives in its site. Perhaps this is the antithesis of the brightly coloured architecture featured in this issue. And perhaps this twentieth-century tradition/trend also goes some way towards answering the question of why architectural education rarely focuses on colour and its effects. Colour is often considered merely as an afterthought, as the domain of the interior designer, outcast with other forms of decoration by Modernists at the beginning of the century. Le Corbusier followed Adolf Loos and echoed the feelings of many at the time when declaring that more civilised societies used less applied decoration.

Once a skill has been lost by a society it is often difficult to revive. Reference to the example of other cultures can invigorate this process, particularly in this age of mass-communication and multiculturalism, though the culture and climate from which inspiration is taken should also be considered. The use of colour in architecture today is often from sunny climates – is this by accident? Mexican Luis Barragán has been the mentor for many architects keen to utilise colour within their designs. Barragán's architecture catches wind and water more effectively than the ideas and anxieties of the moment, but its virtue lies in just that. Colour is an essential as opposed to a decorative dimension of his work. While many architects have been inspired by him there is a particular group of Californian architects whose work echoes his. Mark Mack never hesitates to use colours, sometimes with almost random distribution, though they are always matched with materials to give them true substance and identity. Ricardo Legoretta is also a wonderful example of a 'colour architect'. He understands the effects that colour can have on architectural planes which he carries forward with the traditions of the 20th-century muralist painters. Colour accentuates shape and yet can actively deny the real mass of a building form. Legoretta colours the walls bright yellow, sky blue or vivid magenta in apparent defiance of their massive reality, spreading a rich work of art across entire walls, they are not polemical but contemporary abstract art. They are strong statements of a proud architecture.

It is not only in bright locations that such implementations of colour exist. Even within the rainy bounds of London architects CZWG persist in the use of bright colours in significant locations. Their public toilets finished in bright turquoise tile were built in West London, despite being in a strict conservation area and requiring the raising of extra money by the residents.

Perhaps it is necessary to have strict rules for the application of colour within architecture. Perhaps it is the lack of such guidance in architectural schools which has led to the lack of colour in some areas followed by a flood of bizarre colour arrangements with the onslaught of Post-Modernism in the 80s. In 1856, Owen Jones, a British architect, set out a series of principles to be observed when using colours. These went right back to basics and included explanations of the effects of colour and instructions on where to place certain colours in relation to others to achieve desired effects. He felt that no improvement would take place unless principles were defined and adhered to and the public at large were better educated. Certainly a greater emphasis could be placed on teaching the qualities of colour within architectural schools.

Michael Lancaster discusses principles of the perception of colour in the landscape, ideas which will be expanded upon in his volume on *Colourscape* to be published later in the year. The role of colour in the city is tackled by Galen Minah who charts the use of colour by architects, despite a variety of architectural styles this century, and Cliff Moughtin, Taner Oc and Steven Tiesdell present common conceptions and misconceptions on the theory of using colour. Tom Porter notes architects' resistance to the use of colour in their work and compares this with the public's reaction which is inevitably favourable.

The projects selected demonstrate the variety of uses and locations in which colour can be implemented with pleasing and popular results. The colours may take their cue from the environment, as with Legorreta or Tomás Taveira's General Assembly Building Extension, or contrast with it, as with Ton Voet's Delta School and Ortner and Ortner's Maxx Hotel.

Perhaps the selection of buildings here will inspire architects and encourage them to avoid playing safe with neutral colours.

Colour in the architecture of Legorreta Architects

TOM PORTER
COLOUR IN THE LOOKING GLASS

While researching colour preference at Oxford Brookes University I became aware of a similar project at Cambridge University. Whilst I was testing humans, the Cambridge University project focused on the colour preference of Rhesus monkeys – which possess a colour vision very similar to humans. The results of the two tests were very similar – in descending order: blue, red, green, purple, orange and yellow.

Our tests evolved into studies of colour preference and context. For example, one test was carried out in conjunction with Rowntree Mackintosh which produced some specially coloured Smarties and discovered the popularity of the blue Smartie. It took Rowntree Mackintosh six years to pluck up the courage to mass-produce this highly popular colour.

The preference for blue crops up in a survey by *The Pulse*, the newsletter of the American Roper Organisation, where almost 50 per cent of those tested named blue as their favourite colour, with red in second place. Blue is also America's best-selling car colour, with red cars in second place. Meanwhile, Britain's top auto manufacturers identify blue, red, and white as consistently holding the inside track for the top sales positions.

The fact that many architects seem reluctant to use colour fascinates me. I believe this is something to do with their education and is best illustrated by two ways of viewing of the Parthenon in Greece. The first is an architectural perception that sees this temple as a monochromatic essay in proportional excellence. The second perception sees it as it actually appeared on its opening day in 447BC. Then, it was completely covered in paint and gilding. Both interpretations – the architectural and the Ancient Greek, concern concepts of purity. The coloured version involves 'purity' because this is the very meaning of the work 'Parthenon'.

A dramatic influence on architectural colour came in the 1970s when artists began to use buildings as canvases. In the early 1980s, we conducted two surveys at Oxford: one compared responses of both lay people and architects to powerfully coloured buildings. This found a remarkable enthusiasm among the public for a more richly coloured built environment – much more so than the architects in our survey would allow.

A second survey investigated the incidence of colour teaching in educational design programmes in the UK. This found only two in operation at that time. However, a more recent survey of architecture and design schools finds a vast increase in colour education – an improvement that suggests colour is now being considered as an important facet of the design process. A study of how architectural colour is used by architects seems to break down into a series of functions: first, there is its symbolic use – a function that spans from the colours of the Parthenon to an ocean-linked B&I Ferry Terminal in Dublin. Another function seems to respond to those psychologists who plead for a greater environmental clarity. This uses colour coding as a 'supergraphic' to discriminate between the forms or main working part of a building. However, a third function takes us back to one of the earliest uses of colour on buildings. That is, the blending of architectural form into its setting. This is a kind of colourful camouflage. The fourth function is the complete opposite. This colour approach seeks to detach the building from its setting and uses its colour to decorate or to refer to concepts and ideas that exist beyond its setting.

However, whatever the function of colour in buildings, the choice of hues together with the intensity of their variables – value (colour plus black) and chroma (colour strength), seem to respond also to a kind of colour fashion. This in turn appears to reflect a spirit of the time. Furthermore, within this constant 'recycling' of the colour experience one can detect high points, such as in the brilliance of hues used by Owen Jones in Paxton's Crystal Palace in the 1850s and, again, on the Art Deco 'temples' of the 1930s. This continuously shifting fascination for different parts of the spectrum can be interpreted as an exploratory journey through the world of colour; an adventure that can also be documented on a decade-by-decade basis.

The 1960s

This decade opened with a fascination for black, white, and metallic neutrals. These were expressed in the fashions of the period, including those from the design houses of Cardin, Courreges, and Quant. Meanwhile, fine art was engaged in the scientific study of optical illusions – Op Art confining itself to the disturbance caused by visual fields using intense and geometric combinations of black and white. This mania for achromatics was, of course, a direct reflection of a science fiction fantasy – a recurrent theme is fashion and product design in which we become bedazzled by the glitter and gadgetry of black and silver electronic products. Indeed, the mathematical and hard-edged mood of the first part of the decade simply responded to the advent of space travel and our mental journey into outer space.

Meanwhile, the second half of the 1960s witnessed a complete change in our colour mood. This followed the birth of the package holiday in Great Britain, the possibility of cheap travel to faraway places coinciding with a thirst for the experience of other cultures. Consequently, the bright organic hues of ethnic folk cultures entered the British home. Much of this colour display centred on Indian culture, an interest that recycled an earlier focus on ancient Egyptian decoration, which in the 1930s had followed the discovery of Tutankhamen's tomb. However, this half of the decade also saw the emergence of the hippie and an hallucinogenic drug-inspired psychedelia that represented our journey into the inner space of our mind.

The 1970s

The 1970s saw our return to a science fiction fantasy but this time expressed in an exposed technology. We became deeply interested in how things worked. The need to confront the working parts of a complex technology saw visible mechanisms, such as exposed wristwatch architecture where the hitherto hidden work-ing parts of buildings became exposed – their mechanical guts being spilled directly into the street for all to see. Perhaps the most famous example of the time was the Centre Pompidou, in Paris. However, this adventure into a high technology had to be clarified. To do so, bold primary and secondary colours were enlisted to diagram individual elements and the concept of 'colour-coding' had arrived. These 'high tech' expressions of black, white, and the bold primary colours were also found in fashion and product design, where the influence of a revival of interest in the work of De Stijl designers brought slabs of red, black, blue, and yellow to our lifestyles.

The 1980s

The early 1980s saw a new mood which, albeit short-lived, accompanied an economic boom. This triggered the beginning of the 'pastel phase' – a period when fashion hues became mixed with white to represent 'upmarket' and 'sophisticated taste'. Pastel colours spread quickly and became associated with lifestyle, a concept that involved various groups of colours aimed at differ-ent attitudes or fantasies of living, such as 'nostalgia', 'natural', 'sporty', 'classic', and 'ethnic'. Subdued colour ranges became co-ordinated across all kinds of products associated with a particular 'style of living', from clothes to cars and from interiors to luggage.

Fed by such popular television programmes as the highly influ-ential *Miami Vice*, the pastel trend became truly international in spirit. For example, the co-ordinated hues of men's and women's clothing in New York in 1985 appeared in the same year and in the same colours for new automobile models launched at the Frankfurt, Paris, and Tokyo Motor Shows. Colours hitherto consid-ered suitable only for baby clothes were worn by adults and were even used on Parker Pens and aggressive machines like Honda motorcycles and Fiat cars.

However, this quest for status through colour was also tinged with a nostalgia for the past. The search for 'real bread' and 'real ale' was embedded in the concept of an idealised rural life and a 'cosy country cottage' style – a need being fed by the fashion and interior designs of Laura Ashley, Conran's Habitat, and Next. The 'natural' theme also saw the success of ICI's Natural Whites, a range of white paint tinted with a hint of colour. There was also the rise of 'Muffin,' a soft beige pastel that became Britain's best-selling paint colour (after white) of the decade.

An international expression of pastel colours was stimulated by the painted facades and interiors of the Post-Modernist reaction to the drabness of a Modernist creed. Highly influential were the more figurative designs of Michael Graves, whose Mediterranean palette became transposed to product and electronic goods. This colour mood was quickly adopted in the Japanese electronic industry, which launched pastel-pink televisions, powder-blue telephone handsets, soft grey and yellow transistor radios, as

FROM ABOVE: Smarties, Rowntree Mackintosh; Parthe-non, Greece, drawing detail. As it would have looked when first built in 447BC.

well as steam irons highlighted in pale yellow, blue, and pink.

The 1990s

News of the discovery by British scientists in 1987 of a hole in the earth's ozone layer had sunk into the public conscience by the end of the 1980s. Issues such as deforestation, global warming, and chemical pollution caused a deep concern for the future of the planet. By functioning as the watchdog of this deterioration, the hue of the green movement became the target of high fashion. While this colour association found 'responsible' yet gullible reactions to environmental awareness – green representing lead-free gasoline and the previously mentioned ascendancy of the green-coloured automobile – green had become adopted again as the symbol of survival. This was simply an updating of the fertility hue found in antiquity from the green-painted floors of ancient Egyptian temples to symbolise the fertile meadows of the Nile, to the myth of the Green Man and the Lincoln Green of Robin Hood.

The age of 'greenness' has also started to modify traditional colour meanings. It was predicted in 1990 that white, traditionally associated with the packaging of such refined white foodstuffs as salt, flour, and sugar, would be replaced by earth brown, in reaction to the disturbing environmental effect of chlorine bleaching. However, by 1991 the 'back to nature' fashion saw earthy browns, terracottas, golds, and silvers accompanying moss greens, grass greens, and leaf greens widely used in interior and product design.

However, by looking back in order to peer into the future, this approach is necessarily broad in scope. Obviously, there are countless sub-plots (smaller eddies and currents of colour trend, which are detected on a season-to-season basis within the larger waves of predilection). For instance, in focusing on colour trends in interior design with particular reference to paint, my work has involved the monitoring of seasonal paint colour sales as one means of plotting the rise and decline of individual hues, but this has always been conducted within the broader approach. However, within each branch of the manufacturing industries, each process of colour prediction aims for the same result. Indeed, as these industries rely upon accuracy of forecast for their survival so do forecasters rely on accuracy for theirs.

As we move on through the 1990s, our quest for survival has demanded environmentally safe pigments and dyes for the more variegated and chromatically adventurous colour ranges that have followed the green phase. However, several forecasters predict a return to the science fiction dream in the years immediately preceding the year 2000. In other words, a renewed interest in the subdued hues of blacks, greys, grey-blues, and grey red-blues will hallmark the dying years of the present decade. This seems to point to nothing more than a pause in neutral before the onset of the next century – a lull before the storm of exuberance and innovation that is bound to accompany the thrust into the new millennium. After all, we still live today in the wake of the shock waves triggered by the exhilaration in design at the beginning of the twentieth century.

Tom Porter is a colour specialist and senior lecturer at Oxford Brookes University School of Architecture. He is the author of numerous books on colour and design including The Colour Eye.

Traynor O'Toole Partnership, B&I Ferry Terminal, Dublin

GALEN MINAH

READING FORM AND SPACE: THE ROLE OF COLOUR IN THE CITY

Colour in architecture, in architectural drawings and in the facades and interior spaces of built projects, has been a characteristic focus in work from the early 70s at the birth of Post-Modernism through the current late Modernist and Deconstructivist phases which dominate the architectural media. The most published architects in the last fifteen years have been highly skilled in graphic abilities; some being accomplished painters and graphic artists, whose most memorable work is not their buildings but their splendid presentations. Michael Graves, Zoe Zenghelis, Zaha Hadid, the models of Frank O Gehry, and the bright red follies for Parc de la Villette in Paris by Bernard Tschumi are familiar to every architecture student. The current wave of interest in colour began when Robert Venturi sanctioned American subculture, ignored the restraints on colour from early Modernism and used colour in architecture as imagery in much the same way as roadside advertising.[1]

Much of the work of the 90s, particularly the recent work of Peter Eisenman and Bernard Tschumi – architects associated with the Deconstruction movement in architecture – has used theories of language and meaning as arguments for their conceptual design in which ambiguities, contradictions, and multiple meanings are translated through their interpretation into architectural form. Colour is strongly integral as a component of this form-language, but its rationale is often part of the designer's own subjective language of colour.[2]

In academic circles there are personalities who are noted colourists, such as Robert Slutsky at the Department of Fine Arts, University of Pennsylvania, and John Hejduk at Cooper-Union in New York City, who have been influential in stimulating an interest in colour among architecture students, but their teaching is often very esoteric, and related strongly to their own ideas developed through their painting.

Although colour has been used in architecture for the last 20 years, colour theory as part of an objective methodology for design in which colour becomes part of a conceptual understanding of architectural form in the design process, or is used as a critical tool for evaluation, seldom enters architectural design education.

It is important to look closely at the formative period of the early Modern movement, particularly at the attitudes toward colour and architecture, and examine the ways in which colour was incorporated in the theory, teaching, and production of those times.[3]

A schism in approach to design education known as the 'Norm vs Form debate' took place during the Deutsche Werkbund Exhibition of 1914. 'Norm' represented the belief in the development and refinement of prototypes in architecture and industrial design; and 'Form' represented the creative sovereignty of the individual artist.

This controversy carried into the early years of the Dessau Bauhaus. Johannes Itten was an artist and colour theorist who sided with the artistic, anti-authoritarian 'Form' side of the argument. Itten established a very important teaching document in his book *Art of Colour*, which is still used in teaching colour theory to artists and architects. Itten taught the basic design course at the Bauhaus, in which his teaching methods were subjective, very inner-directed and focused on individual creativity. Itten was interested in how personality could be revealed through colour exercises, and had a somewhat mystical approach to colour and design. His anti-authoritarian beliefs often clashed with the strongly rational approach of Bauhaus director and architect Walter Gropius. When Gropius proclaimed his support for professors in the industrial production and craft design faction of the Bauhaus, Itten resigned. He was replaced by László Moholy-Nagy, a Hungarian artist with constructivist leanings who took over the basic design course. Moholy-Nagy practised 'programmed art', and was well known for his 'telephone pictures' which were executed by calling colour specifications to a factory supervisor who then produced the work of art in enamelled steel.[4] Moholy-Nagy fitted in very well with Gropius's rational objectives, and he became a powerful influence in the Bauhaus.

At the same time, *Neue Sachlichkeit*, or 'New Objectivity', emerged as the intellectual basis for design theory in the late 1920s. New Objectivity practitioners sought to make the design process a highly rational one, stressing materiality, economy, and function, and divesting designed artefacts of any ideal implications. New Objectivity was the foundation for many early twentieth-century movements in design such as Suprematism and Neo-Plasticism or De Stijl .

The Dutch De Stijl movement was an important accomplishment in the use of colour as a tool in theoretical approaches to architectural form. The best known members of this movement were the artists Piet Mondrian and Theo van Doesburg, who became the prime spokesman for the movement, and Gerrit Rietveld, an architect who produced some of the only built objects of this period. Their lofty goal was, 'to work through the arts to achieve an ideal future when all walls that separate men would be broken down, society integrated and capable of constructing an urban environment of abstract forms.'[5] These artist architects saw the three-dimensional properties of mass and volume as antithetical to their movement, and they attempted to counteract and destroy these formal characteristics through the use of colour. Their methodology was to use primary colours, white and green planes of colour defined by black borders, displacing corners and the boundaries of floors and ceilings with these colour planes, thus changing the volumetric characteristics of architectural space. In its place, one experienced floating planes of colour, some advancing, some receding, dissolving all the references to cubic volume and becoming an assemblage of spatial effects created by colour juxtapositions.[6]

De Stijl was a dramatic development in the use of colour as both an integral part of the design process and as a tool for the creation of a new spatial experience. No other movement had employed colour as a conceptually spatial idea to this extent and

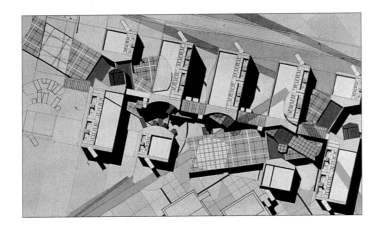

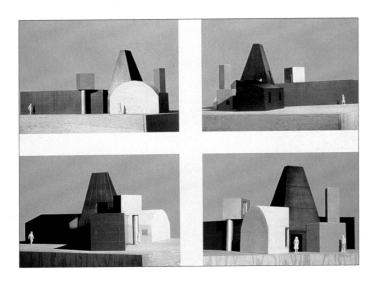

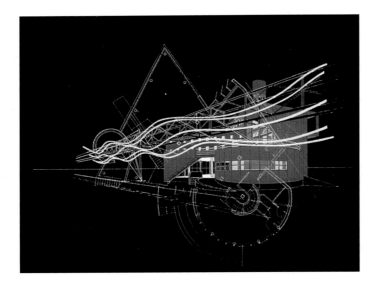

FROM ABOVE: Peter Eisenman, University of Frankfurt Bio-centrum; Frank O Gehry, Winton House, Wayzata, Minnesota; Bernard Tschumi, Parc de la Villette, Paris

none had recognised and used in practice the destructuring capability of colour.

Other movements employing colour as a basis for their conceptual design were Constructivism, in which colour played a symbolic role,[7] and Expressionism. The Expressionists were artists and architects who saw their creative role as a calling to save society through their inspired artistic achievements. Colour for the Expressionists was powerfully emotive and highly individual and subjective, as seen in the architecture of Hans Poelzig and Hans Scharoun.[8]

Le Corbusier was influenced by De Stijl, particularly in his use of colour in Pessac Housing of 1929. With the artist Ozenfant, Le Corbusier established Purism, which among other influences, brought machine aesthetics to the attention of contemporary architects. The colour white was a dominant theme in the architecture influenced by Purism particularly in the 1930s; later, white surfaces and structural members became a characteristic of the International Style. Mies van der Rohe and Walter Gropius were influenced by Le Corbusian theories, but their work was characteristically restrained in the use of colour except for the qualities of colour and texture in unadorned materials such as steel, glass, concrete, masonry and stone. Colour was considered ornamental and thus superficial when applied purposely.

Gropius and Mies went to the United States as teachers in the late 1930s, and their influence in architectural education is still felt in the design studios of professors today, who were students of these two men. This accounts in part for the continuation of their attitudes about colour in US architectural education today.

Except for the teaching of the early Bauhaus and the brief emergence of colour in the movements described above, colour theory and teaching has been considered supplemental to the mainstream of architectural education. Architecture students in the United States have few courses in colour theory or studios which focus on colour in architectural design. Rarely is a course offered in which colour in design and the relationship of form and colour to architecture is the focus of the instruction.

An exception to this is a course offered by Christopher Alexander at the University of California at Berkeley, in which Alexander's pattern language is expanded to employ the use of colour by studying cultural precedents for the use of colour in various spaces based on functional similarities.[9]

Colour in student work, for the most part, remains a matter of individual expression most often influenced by journal graphics and high quality photographs of built projects in which the colouration is often exaggerated. A student's involvement with colour at the University of Washington Department of Architecture is entirely elective. Occasionally students from fine arts who matriculate for a professional degree in architecture have some knowledge of colour theory, but for the most part colour remains a matter of individual taste. Colour issues are rarely discussed in a design studio review, and then almost never on an objective basis.

The challenge is to bring colour theory into a conceptual framework where its relevance is part of the design process. This challenge has become the point of departure for these investigations in colour-form interactions, and the subject for a number of graduate architectural design studios. Colour theory is used in these classes as a conceptual design tool to expand the means for clarifying the figural or hierarchical nature of building form. Colour theory is also used in the analytical or interpretative phase of the process as a critical tool in examining the integral relationships between the parts and the whole.

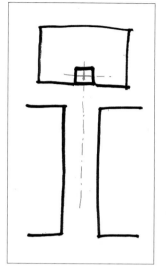

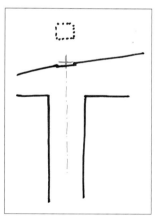

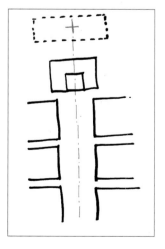

FROM ABOVE, L to R: Tower diagram I; streetscape, England; tower diagram II; streetscape, Liverpool, England; tower diagram III; Grand Central Station and the Pan Am Building, New York

Most formal analysis dismisses colour as transitory or treats it as a specific issue in the analysis of form. The preferred media for analytic studies are black and white drawings and photographs for elevational and perspectival studies. When colour is introduced it is not used in the critique of building form. Colour, however, is a powerful factor in the reading of form, as seen in the work of the De Stijl movement, and it is a major factor in clarifying the figure-ground relationships. Diagramming techniques used in formal analysis reveal the order of figure-ground, and these can be amplified by colour studies.

It is also clear that the perception of spatial phenomena is due in part to colour contracts, through juxtaposition of colour surfaces, and to the effects of atmospheric perspective upon colour. Certain colour phenomena such as these fall into categories that are recognisable and thus generalisable. These categories can be represented as part of the 'familiar' and 'general' world of colour interactions, and can also be represented through diagrammatic strategies. As with the formal analysis of buildings, a colour field can be named using the same terminology as architectural forms: centre, perimeter, figure and ground. For example, an abstract painting can be analysed, diagrammed, and interpreted in much the same way as a work of architecture, although colour juxtapositions become the only formal elements.

Since we understand the architectural diagram by means of black and white, solid and void, we neglect atmospheric reality in which colour is the variable which complicates and enriches the experience of figure, ground, solid and void. Colour has the capacity to clarify the figural components of form or confuse or obfuscate these elements causing multiple readings of architectural form.

Three examples of how building form and colour contrasts interact can be illustrated with these views of towers in an urban environment. The first example shows a distant tower as the clear terminus of an axis defined by the street and flanking buildings, and a diagram of the important plan relationships. Colour contrast does not play a major role in this view, although the relationship between the perimeter walls, building types, and the tower could be strengthened by colour.

The second example illustrates a distant tower, a square and an uncertain connection between the two. The diagram shows one set of relationships from a plan view, but the perspectival view illustrates another interpretation. The bold facade created with strong colour contrast becomes clearly figural and takes the focus of the axis. The tower becomes a background element in the three-dimensional view.

The third example illustrates another clear tower-axis relationship in the plan diagram and in three dimensions. The tower is Grand Central Station in New York City, a major landmark and node in the city. The station's formal setting in the city was changed with the construction of the Pan American Building in the 1960s. This tower receives the attention of the axis of the avenue, rather than Grand Central Station. Colour contrast might alter the relationship between the Station and the Pan Am Building and restore the Station to its focal role at the end of the avenue by using a colour juxtaposition that makes the station figural and 'advances' it spatially.

An example of the interaction of building form with colour is the Portland Building in Portland, Oregon, by Michael Graves. If we compare the architect's line rendering of the building which portrays a clear cubic mass with delineated parts with the actual building, there are substantial differences. The actual building's

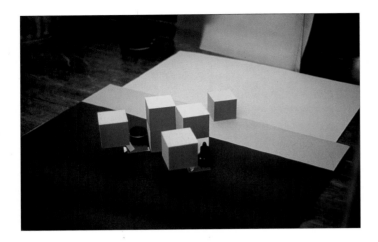

FROM ABOVE: Cube project by student; Michael Graves, Portland Building, Portland, Oregon; Michael Graves, Portland Building sketch

colours reveal another interpretation of the nature of the building. Here the cubic volume appears to bracket a second volume which appears as a dark mass in the centre of the building. Thus the actual volumetric characteristic of the building appears quite different from the drawn work.

The work which follows is a composite of experiments, observations, and student projects from a number of design studios taught by me, beginning in 1980, at the University of Washington. The students were graduate students in the professional degree program in architecture.

The first investigation was to explore the spatial effect of colour and create optical illusions using this effect in three-dimensional form. Students constructed three inch by three inch paper cubes with single planes of colour on their faces. Through colour juxtapositions and the spatial effect created by these juxtapositions students were asked to arrange these cubes in space and photograph them from a point of view which would create an optical illusion, misrepresenting the actual positions in space which the cubes occupied. It was interesting to note in these exercises the power and ambiguous characteristic of black. Black can be figural either as a solid or a void, and can easily deceive the eye as to its actual position in space. A black object in front of a lighter background can advance dramatically toward the viewer, or appear as a void in the background.

In the next exercise students were asked to find and photograph examples of the spatial effect in the urban environment with particular attention to the figure to ground interactions. These examples were numerous, and the variety of spatial effects observed were apparent in large spatial contexts as well as in fine detail. For example, light columns in slight relief on a darker background appeared from a distance as free-standing columns. Warmer coloured buildings appeared closer to the viewer than cooler buildings at approximately the same distance. The tops of towers from street level could deceive the eye as to their actual positions in space if colour contrasts were present.

In these initial studies we noticed specifically two factors which affected colour in urban settings: the importance of daylighting and climatic conditions on the perceived colour effects within the city, and the dominant presence of highly saturated colours in the environment. These two factors became subjects for further study in later design studio courses.

To study the effects of daylighting and climatic conditions upon colour in Seattle, we first photographed colour samples on bright and overcast days to observe colours which changed significantly with these conditions. We also photographed single family residential areas that had a variety of colour juxtapositions and could be viewed from a distance. Photography was done in differing weather conditions, and at different times of the day. From these exercises we observed the changes in the reds in the urban environment, particularly brick, in sunshine and in overcast skies. In sunshine, the red-orange hues dominated, usually making the building figural as the reds advanced when contrasted against a cooler field. On overcast days, the reds became dull and cool and retreated, into the background, changing sometimes from figure to ground spatially.

Blues, on the other hand, became vibrant and appeared more saturated on overcast days. This also was true of hues that contain blue such as blue-green, red-violet, etc. Yellows also became vibrant on overcast days, and colours with yellow components such as green could alternate between blue-green and yellow-green in differing light conditions. Guided by these initial

FROM ABOVE: First Street and Pike Street, Seattle, showing the focus on reds in buildings; First Street and Pike Street, Seattle on a cloudy day; warehouse in Seattle, showing the focus on saturated colour (red) at a distance.

observations, we photographed a number of buildings and objects in the red, blue and yellow range of colours on sunny, overcast and rainy days.

Another investigation focused on highly saturated colours on buildings within the city to observe their spatial effect. Of particular interest was to see how atmospheric perspective changed these colours and what spatial effects occurred at varying distances. Observations were made in different lighting conditions and these were photographed. Saturated reds and yellows were the most obvious colours on buildings observed. Both reds and yellows advanced dramatically from every point of view and seemed less affected by atmospheric perspective than the surrounding buildings. The strength of highly saturated colours, particularly on large surfaces such as building facades is obvious from this study, and these colours have an ability to exaggerate the spatial effect, advancing toward the viewer in nearly every example we observed.

In Washington DC, the Capitol Building, the White House, and the Washington Monument are all white, achieving figural status against the darker landscape, and advancing spatially. Against the sky the contrast is softened and makes the buildings appear to float in space. White also reveals detail in shadow often making the building appear larger than it really is. Buildings with a combination of very large scale contrasted with repetitive small scale elements make the building appear larger, exemplified in the drawings of the French neo-classical architect Ledoux. Many of the flanking institutional buildings are off-white, giving them equal status with one another, but of lesser rank than the primary buildings.

In comparing the planning of governmental and major institutional buildings in Seattle to Washington DC there is little similarity. In Seattle most institutional buildings are treated no differently from commercial buildings, occupying the same block pattern. There is no hierarchical intervention such as a central park, a mall, or a purposeful axis. The plan of the city reveals little information about where the governmental buildings are and how they achieve their status. In fact, they have no separate status: they occupy the same sized blocks as the commercial buildings, and have no plazas nor any special height.

Seattle contains a concentration of skyscrapers in the central business district where commercial, governmental and institutional buildings are located. The towers themselves are dominated by one massive black building, the Columbia Centre, the highest tower in the city. The coloration is designed to show minimal shadow and little detail, thereby creating a black monolith of great power within the city. The figural strength of this building is not because of its height alone or its position in the city but by its colour. However, it is really only another commercial office tower, which in most American cities are really background buildings in terms of their civic importance. The Seattle City Hall huddles at its feet directly adjacent to the Seattle Public Library which is also dwarfed, as are the court houses and the art museum a few blocks away.

In a design studio focusing on colour and urban form, students were given a building design project in the central business district near the Columbia Centre. As a sketch problem, students made a large painting from photographs of a view of the Columbia Centre in its urban context. Each student was asked to change the colour scheme of the Columbia Centre and paint an overlay to be attached to the original painting. It was interesting to see how the centre of gravity of skyline comprised of all the towers together was changed when the Columbia Centre was light grey or

 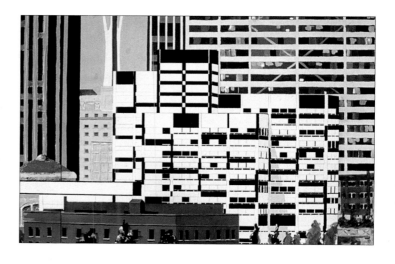

ABOVE: Washington Monument, Washington DC; CENTRE: Seattle skyline showing black towers; Columbia Centre, Seattle, student project, rendering by John Kope; BELOW: King County Jail and Skybridge, Seattle, colour study by student Ann van Dyne; colour study by student Reese Kaufman.

silver and softened by the skyscape.

In the second part of the quarter, students were given a building design project for an office tower on a site in the central business district near the Columbia Centre. The new tower was not as high as the Columbia Centre but would be in a prominent position in front of the Columbia Centre when viewed approaching the city from the east, west or south. The students were asked to select colour schemes for their new towers which approached the figural status of the Columbia Centre.

The most interesting resulting design was a white tower which used colour to exaggerate its own height and stood as a strong counterpoint to the black tower. A more neutral colour scheme would have joined other neutral towers and become part of the background. A dark tower would become one of the family with the Columbia Centre and other dark towers, but a smaller sibling.

Another design project in the vicinity of the Columbia Centre addressed the new county jail, built adjacent to the major north-south freeway and just on the edge of the central business district at the south end of the city. As one approaches the city from the south, the jail becomes a gateway building. The new jail is a block away from the Columbia Centre and near City Hall and the County Courthouse. The jail is designed to look like a neutral beige office building. Through clever coloration, dark concrete panels give the appearance of large glass windows, however, at the base of these panels is a five inch slit which is the only real window to the cells behind. At night these slits become visible, and the building becomes a looming dark object with eerie thin slits of light, contrasted to the lofty, fully lit office towers.

Tight security is required when prisoners are moved from the jail to the county courthouse two blocks away. To provide this security a high skybridge extends from the top floor of the jail across a street over an entire block at the roof of an adjacent building, across another street, and into the courthouse. The bridge, intended to be innocuous and avoid notice, instead becomes a figural foreign object, and thus a sinister intrusion into the fabric of the city.

Students were asked to select a point of view from photographs which included the new jail and bridge with the city behind. A mural of this view was painted by the class. This exercise gave the students experience in mixing the greys and beiges which make up much of the urban palette. The students were then asked to take a point of view about the relationship of a jail to the commercial center of the city, and express this point of view in colouristic terms. This was recognised as an abstract exercise, knowing that a project like this in reality would need to consider more than one point of view.

Many students chose to accept the institution for what it was without disguising it. These projects made the building more figural in nature and treated the dark concrete panels as planes of colour rather than disguised as windows. Most solutions attempted to break the dominant scale and figural nature of the bridge with varying planes of colour. Some experimented with hues complementary to the warm grays and browns of the surrounding buildings for the purpose of creating a colour harmony with the urban context, but appearing as clearly distinct from the other buildings. The most unusual design was done by a student who abstracted the pattern of windows from the surrounding towers, and in bold black and white rectangles de-structured the cubic volume of the jail into a collage of fragments which blended with the rectangular patterns of the windows in the surrounding buildings.

In all these exercises, students used an analytical process to explore the relationship between their designs and the larger urban context. As part of this process, they made colour decisions that would clarify the formal and spatial properties of the designed buildings. This inevitably led to a broader understanding of how colour contrasts and, in particular, the spatial effect of colour become components in figure and ground and the perception of three-dimensional space. The students also learned that colour is part of the experiential nature of architectural awareness, and that its relevance in the design process is one of clarifying, complementing and enhancing rather than as an independent study.

Formal analysts feel it is impossible to fully 'know' a building. It can only be understood as a group of diverse abstractions. Likewise, it is impossible to fully 'know' a city, but the complexities and ambiguities which characterise the 'reading' of form and space are truly enriched by the diversity of colour, giving great variety to the creative interpretation of the city.

Galen Minah is Associate Professor of Architecture at the University of Washington.

Notes
1 Galen Minah, 'Colour Language', *Arcade* (Seattle), 1984, p3.
2 Peter Eisenman and Bernard Tschumi, *Deconstruction*, Architectural Design (New York), 1989, pp154-191.
3 Kenneth Frampton, *Modern Architecture, A Critical History* (London), 1992.
4 Frampton, *Modern Architecture*, pp124-126.
5 N Troy, 'De Stijl Manifesto', *The De Stijl Environment* (Boston), 1983, pp5-6.
6 Troy, *De Stijl Environment*, p83.
7 Chernikhov, J, 'The Harmony of Colours', *Deconstruction*, Architectural Design (New York), 1989, pp56-59.
8 W Pehnt, *Expressionist Architecture* (London), 1973, pp34-47.
9 C Alexander, *The Linz Café* (New York and Vienna), 1981, created an illusion of increased depth and occupied space beyond.

CLIFF MOUGHTIN, TANER OC AND STEVEN TIESDELL

COLOUR IN THE CITY

There is a renewed interest in the use of colour, one of the most effective methods of decorating the city. Colour should be used to strengthen the image of the city by giving emphasis to features such as landmarks, by developing colour schemes which are associated with particular districts, streets or squares and by colour coding street furniture.

There is great potential for polychromatic colour effects in the built environment. For much of this century the subject of colour in the city was not a matter for serious attention. A classical ideal, subscribed to by many designers, mistakenly associated with the architecture and sculpture of Ancient Greece, sees colour in architecture as a product only of natural finishes. The standing remains of ancient civilisations which have survived the ravages of time have been bleached of their original colouring by sun, wind and rain. They have, therefore, functioned as a monochromatic source of inspiration. To many the discovery that the great monuments of antiquity were stained or painted with bright pigments has proved quite unacceptable, particularly to those with a puritanical reverence for the expression of the inherent appearance of natural materials. The facts, however, are quite clear; 'Statuary was deeply dyed with garish pigments. The marble figure of a woman found on the Athenian Acropolis was tinctured red, green, blue and yellow. Quite often statues had red lips, glowing eyes made of precious stones and even artificial eyelashes.'[1] The Greek temple from the point of view of colour was closer in feeling to the Chinese temple, than to those pure but lifeless nineteenth-century copies found in many European cities.

The love of colour survives in the modern world. The church in its vestments retains a strong link with the past symbolic use of colour while colourful vivacity occasionally breaks out in the guise of the latest Parisian or Italian fashions in women's clothes. In the environment colour was kept alive by those not schooled in the centres of artistic excellence – the working class in the suburban home, the art of the bargee, the gypsy or fairground artist. In this spirit are the monuments to Art Deco of the late 1920s and 1930s. Such buildings as those by Wallis, Gilbert and Partners for suburban London fall neatly within this populist genre. Within the Modern Movement important experiments with colour were carried out. The De Stijl group in Holland in the early 1920s was one such group. While Mondrian used pure colours and white on canvas, containing them in a black grid of simple rectangles, Rietveld, following similar principles, decorated the internal and external planes of his architecture. Other notable modern exponents of colour in the environment include Le Corbusier who used flashes of intense primary colours to contrast with the white geometric frame of his architecture.

The legacy of the dogmatic views of Ruskin and the priggish taste in colour of those who followed abandoned the field of polychromy to the engineer. It was the engineer who embellished and protected with paint the ironwork of bridges, the coach work of the railway engine and the working parts of industrial and agricultural machinery. Arguably it was not until the building of the Pompidou Centre by Richard Rogers and Renzo Piano that a return was made to the more ancient architectural traditions of environmental colouring.

The natural colours of traditional settlements constructed from local materials delights the eye. The sophisticated and almost pristine colouring of De Stijl gives great intellectual and emotional satisfaction. They are, however, by no means the only ways in which colour can be introduced into the environment. The case being made here is the need for a more catholic and eclectic philosophy of colour in the environment. This is particularly true now when so much urban development is a concrete jungle. Given the current emphasis on sustainability, many local authorities attempt to humanise the built environment with paint, vegetation and sculpture instead of demolishing the concrete jungle.

Theory of colour

Before discussing colour in the environment it is useful to examine the general theory of colour and to define terms used to describe and specify colours. The term colour can be used in two main ways: to describe the hues of the rainbow, the constituent parts into which white light is broken (red, yellow, blue, etc), or, it can be used in its more popular form and include black, white and grey. The last three 'colours' can be obtained as paints for use in the home in the same way as red, blue or green. It is this populist definition of colour which is used in this text. It is, however, important to realise that the designer's use of colour in the environment differs from that of the painter. While following the same principle of colour harmony the urban designer is working in a field where the quality of light varies from city to city, from season to season, and from morning through to late evening. The painter, in his or her studio, attempts to mix and use colour in a constant daylight condition. The results of his or her work is exhibited in a gallery where optimum lighting conditions prevail. The painter has control over his or her palette and can chose to follow theoretical trains of thought in the abstract. The urban designer works with other actors in urban development, each following individual intentions. The urban designer works on a canvas which is three dimensional, of immense scale and in a constant process of growth and decay. The starting point for the urban designer must of necessity be the environment of the place in which he or she is working. Colour theory for the city, therefore, has to be seen in this greater context and used, where that is possible, for decorating the city by creating harmony where none may exist.

There are three sets of primary colours from which the other colours can be made. With light rays, red, green and blue (blue-violet) will form other hues when mixed. Red and green will form yellow: green and blue will form turquoise; red and blue will form magenta. Light primaries are additive so that all three light primaries when combined reform to produce white.

With pigments, red, yellow and blue are the primary colours which when combined will normally form other hues. Pigments tend to be subtractive, that is, red paint absorbs all light except red which is reflected from the surface. No pigments are pure mixtures, therefore, and combinations tend to deepen or subtract more of the light falling on the surface. A combination of all three pigment primaries will form black or deep brown: most light falling on the surface will be absorbed and very little reflected.

In vision, however, there are four primaries, red, yellow, green and blue. Each of these colours, perceptually, is quite distinct from each other. Any other colours tend towards one of the primaries. That is, a mix of yellow and green would look either 'greenish' or 'yellowish'. All four colours when spun on a wheel or mixed will form grey.

The three sets of primaries of the artist, the scientist and the psychologist, each produce different colour circles. While each colour circle can be used for deciding colour harmonies, this text, for convenience, will follow the traditional circle of the artist based upon the three primary colours: red, yellow and blue.

Figure 1 illustrates the three primary colour circle of the artist. It shows the distribution of primary, secondary and tertiary colours together with the division of the colour spectrum in terms of warm and cool hues. Ives, who brought this particular spectrum to perfection suggested that the red should be magenta (schlor), the yellow should be clear and clean (zanth) and the blue should be turquoise or peacock. These particular primaries when mixed will give a satisfactory spectrum of pure hues.

The use of colour harmony in painting or the built environment is founded on an understanding of simultaneous and successive contrast and of the phenomena of visual colour mixtures. M Chevreul described in his book the effect of simultaneous contrast as follows: 'If we look simultaneously upon two stripes of different tones of the same colour, or upon two stripes of the same tone of different colours placed side by side . . . the eye perceives certain modifications which in the first place influence the intensity of the colour, and in the second, the optical composition of the two juxtaposed colours respectively.'[2]

Figure 2 illustrates simultaneous contrast of brightness. Both greys are identical in brightness but the one seen against black appears lighter than the one seen on the white ground. Light colours will tend to heighten the depth of dark colour and dark colours will tend to make light colours lighter. Where colours of different value or brightness are placed side by side a fluted effect is produced (see figure 3). The edges of each tone will tend to be modified in contrary ways. The effect of 'afterimage' of contrasting colours is also quite noticeable. Figure 4 illustrates this using black and white (see overleaf). The effect of contrast is best demonstrated by staring at a given hue for a short time; when the gaze is transferred to a white wall the appearance or shadow of the opposite hue is stimulated. Referring to the full colour circle the contrasting colours are those that are diametri-

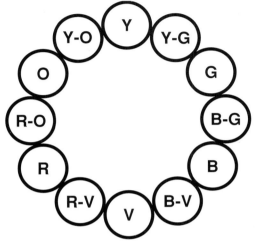

1. The red, yellow and blue colour circle

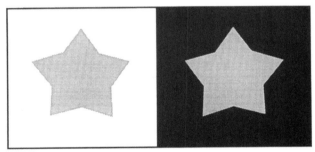

2. Simultaneous contrast: each grey star is identical in brightness

3. Simultaneous contrast: note the 'fluted' effect where the grey tones touch each other

cally opposite on the circle (see figure 5). The after-image of red is blue-green and vice versa; the after-image of yellow is violet and vice versa. Opposite or contrasting colours when used together tend to give brilliance and purity to each other without any change of hue.

Where non-complementary colours are placed side by side they are affected as if tinted by the light of the after-image of the neighbouring colour. When, for example, yellow and orange are placed together the violet after image of the yellow swings the apparent hue of the orange towards red while the blue after-image of the orange will make the yellow appear greenish.

Contrasting effects in value are stronger when light and dark colours are juxtaposed while contrasts in hue are most noticeable when the colours are close in value. However, the size of the colour panels is important for contrasting effects: large panels of colour are most effective for a startling visual contrast, particularly when the contrast is both in value and hue. Strong contrasting colours in minute areas such as spots or lines become diffused by the eye and tend to conceal each other resulting in an overall dullness. Opposite colours, therefore, are most effective in contrast when used in large panels of colour. Adjacent or analogous colours, on the other hand, are best displayed in different minute areas. The effective use of analogous colours can be found in many traditional stone or brick walls. Each stone though from the same quarry is a slightly different hue or shade of hue. They all blend naturally together. The foundation of colour harmony dates from the early nineteenth century and the work of M Chevreul. This theory established certain rules and principles. The first is that individual colours are beautiful in themselves; second, so are tones of the same hue; third, different hues, analogous or closely related on the colour circle, are in an harmonic relationship when they are seen in uniform or closely related tones; finally, complementary hues seen in strongly contrasting tones are also harmonious. Assorted colours when viewed through the medium of a feebly coloured glass take on an harmonic relationship.

The use of colour in the city
Until the nineteenth century, European cities developed slowly employing indigenous materials from their regions for the building envelope. Architectural styles changed but the building materials did not. The constant use of local materials produced streets, squares and whole cities with great visual harmony despite the varied forms. In this way the colour of the city was established and is an aspect of its history which has not been completely submerged by nineteenth- and twentieth-century developments. In Oxford's high street many styles are reflected but all have been unified by scale, material and especially colour. The colour of Oxford is derived from the ochres of the yellow sandstone. In the traditional city there was easy access to cheap earth pigments for painting stucco facades. Even in the nineteenth century it was only the wealthy who could afford the brighter 'imported' or 'foreign' colours for doors and windows. Cities and regions have come to be associated with particular colour ranges: 'For instance, the ochres and reds of Lyons; and, among the blues and reds, the predominance of a "Maria Theresa" yellow in central Vienna. There are also the brickdust reds and Georgian greens of a revamped Savannah, the pinks of Suffolk and Devon cottages, and the brilliant reds, blues and yellows of houses on the Adriatic island of Burano.'[3] The problem posed for the urban designer is how to recapture such colour schemes and give individuality and

distinction back to each centre.

Turin in 1800 set up a Council of Builders to devise and implement a colour plan for the city. The idea was to colour principal streets and squares characterised by a unified architecture in a coordinated scheme. The Council devised a series of chromatic pathways for the major processional routes to Turin's centre, Piazza Castello. The colour scheme for each route was based upon popular city colours and was implemented through permissions given for redecoration applications. It is not known how long the original colour scheme lasted but it was praised by Nietzsche in the late nineteenth century and by Henry James in the early twentieth century.

In his work on colour in the environment Jean Philippe Lenclos has developed the ideas found in Turin's earlier experiment. He has aimed to preserve a sense of place by devising a palette of colours relating to particular localities in France. Lenclos collects colour samples from sites within the region – fragments of paint, materials from walls, doors, shutters, together with natural elements such as moss, lichen, rock and earth. He analyses and structures the colours he finds to form a colour map for the region and a palette for intervention in the built environment.

The lessons that can be learnt from Turin and Lenclos are twofold. First an environmental survey is necessary to establish a colour map of the region or city and from that colour map palettes established as the basis for colour schemes. Second, any colour scheme for a city should be comprehensive and capable of implementation. From earlier sections of the chapter it would seem desirable that any colour scheme established should follow the laws of harmonic colour composition.

There are four different scales on which colour in the city can be seen: the scale of the city or of the district; the scale of the street or square, where colour can create various characteristics or moods depending on adjacent buildings, and at street corners or on diametrically opposed facades; the scale of the individual buildings; and the scale of details – windows, shutters, ironwork, street furnishings. Furthermore colour in streets and on buildings can be seen in four different ways: from the side; from the front; from above; and from below. It can be seen in deep shadow, in conditions of blazing sunshine or harshly against a bright sky. In each condition the same pigment may take on a different shade, tint or tone of the same hue.

Milan is a city which has a clearly defined colour pattern. It is a highly sophisticated and unique use of colour. Cities like Siena, Florence and Bologna depend for their colour on materials such as brick, terracotta and marble. In Florence, for example, dark colours abound including the dark green marble cladding of the cathedral. It is a city of shades and tones. In Siena the light and beautifully decorated cathedral decorates a totally different space from the dark coloured main square and the dark cliff-like streets that connect the cathedral and the main square. Dark brick and terracotta are the colours of the arcaded streets and squares in Bologna where rich gold is splashed on the soffit and arch of vaulted arcades. However, in Milan the experience of colour is quite different: here dark and light colours are juxtaposed. It is a city of light and shade. The highly decorated cathedral provides a white focus to the main square which has dark colours to the south and light pinks to the north. This highlighting of different areas in the city with white marble clad buildings is a theme repeated throughout the city.

In Vienna and Prague, yellow is the colour used to highlight Baroque landmarks. Small Baroque churches usually along narrow streets become visually significant when painted yellow. Colour of such intensity when combined with movements of surface shadows becomes highly decorative without being elaborate. In both Prague and Bratislava elaborately coloured decorations are common in Art Nouveau and Art Deco facades. Colour on buildings from both periods is widely used over facades, and while intricate and pleasing to the casual observer, it nevertheless misses the opportunity for the strategic use of colour and decoration which earlier and more disciplined periods achieved. For instance, the cathedral in Buda is a good example of colour used to highlight a landmark and important symbol of community solidarity. The cathedral stands out in contrast to the dark shades and tones of red, green and yellow used along the nearby medieval streets.

The two most common urban spaces are the street and square. The colour scheme of the street or square may have a considerable effect upon its character and appearance. It can contribute to the unity of the street or square, or it may destroy that unity. In addition, the colours used in the street have in themselves the ability to create character and mood. Taking the street for example, it is possible to emphasise the wall planes of the street by painting them a light tone. Alternatively the volume of the street can be emphasised by colouring the facades the same tone as the dark pavement, or the length of the street could be emphasised by horizontal strips along the facades. The street can also be broken down into units with vertical bands of colouring. Whichever scheme is followed the street should be viewed strategically as an element in the city, a path leading from node to node and interspersed with landmark features and street corners. It is features such as these which should influence the final distribution of colour within the street.

When developing a colour scheme for a building it must first be seen in its strategic relationship with its immediate surroundings. The building's visual function within the city or district should also be established. For example, is the building an important landmark or a closure to a vista? Does the building lie upon an important path with a particular colour coding? Having decided the strategic requirements then the building itself can be examined: if it is rich in decoration it will be articulated with relief – cornices, window frames, niches, projecting bays and oriels, stairwells, corner mouldings, overhanging roofs, balconies, etc. The relief lies in front of the main wall surface and is foreground colour, the wall becomes the ground or background colour. The background may be dark with pale relief or vice versa, but some distinction is necessary for articulation.

When choosing a colour scheme for a building it is the details that are the final constructional elements to receive consideration. It is only when we stop and concentrate the gaze that we notice the details and colour of fixtures and fittings but they are important for the overall effect of the street and where possible if flanking an important route they should be co-ordinated. The three zones of the building, the base, the middle zone and the roof zone, together with the relief and detailing make up the architectural treatment of the street. The planes, projections and ornamental work can be emphasised to create a lively pattern of decoration. In other areas where for strategic or master plan reasons the street can be bland and unassuming then the difference in elements can be masked by the subtle use of shades, tones or tints of the same colour.

Colour is one of the most important aspects of city life: it is one of the main factors in our description of a city's decorative effect. To be fully effective for city decoration requires some strategic policy which sets a colour agenda for the city and its main elements, districts, paths nodes, edges and landmarks. The city image from the point of view of colour is often formed over a long history and also strongly affected by its environmental setting. Determination of colour image requires a sensitive response from the urban designer. A response which should be based on a thorough survey of colour in the local environment. For the remainder of the city, colour can be used to highlight important buildings and landmarks, colour code important paths and give individuality within the overall pattern for important squares and meeting places.

Notes

1   Tom Porter, *Colour Outside*, The Architectural Press (New York), 1982.
2   ME Chevreul, *Principles of Harmony and Contrast of Colours*, reprinted by F Birren, Van Nostrand Reinhold (New York), 1967.
3   T Porter, *Colour Outside*, Architectural Press.

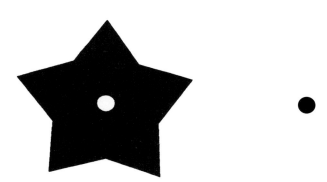

4. After-image: stare at the centre of the black star for several seconds then look steadily at the black dot

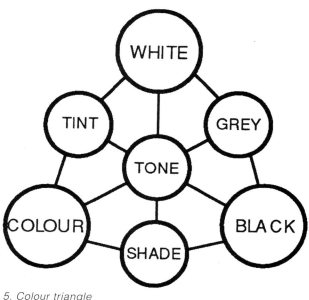

5. Colour triangle

MICHAEL LANCASTER
SEEING COLOUR

Two ways of seeing

We see colour principally in two different ways: as an attribute of objects, and as a separate sensory phenomenon. The surprising fact is that the first, regarded as natural and normal, is based not upon true colour appearance, but upon our experience and visual memory; what we know rather than what we actually 'see'. The 'true' or sensory view of colours is generally regarded as being the prerogative of painters, scientists, and those who work with colour. For the majority of us, most of the time, it is 'the object view' which prevails. The reasons for this are fairly obvious.

In order to negotiate objects and find our way in the world, we need to be able to identify things under a variety of different circumstances and in different light conditions. Colour constancy – in parallel with constancies of size, shape, texture and brightness – enables us to recognise objects and situations which experience has taught us to identify, thus freeing our perceptual faculties for detection of the new and the less unfamiliar. In this there is a direct similarity between the brain and the information processing mechanism of a computer, although the former is infinitely more sophisticated. The visual system is adapted to obtaining a maximum of information with a minimum of effort: that which is not immediately required, or can be taken for granted, can be considered redundant; 'the eye has evolved to see the world in unchanging colour, regardless of [the] always unpredictable, shifting and uneven illumination.'[1]

This dichotomy of colour vision (which Edwin Land suggests may be due to evaluation mechanisms operating within the visual process) seems to suggest answers to a number of questions which arise in attempting to analyse visual perception. First it must surely account for the fact that so many people seem generally unresponsive to colour, except for those credited with aptitude, intuition or 'flair'. It might well account for the common tendency to look so often at paintings in art galleries without registering their colour, and explain why the whole subject of painting can be divided between those whom we recognise as 'good colourists' and those for whom the academic process is more important. There is, for example, an accepted distinction between those schools of painting based upon drawing, such as the Florentine; and those for which colour was predominant, such as the Venetians. Ingres, writing in defence of the academic system claimed; ' . . . drawing is everything, the whole of art lies there. The material processes of painting are very easy and can be learnt in a week or so.'[2]

Such relegation of the subject to the level of a child's colouring book is not untypical, and could well be applied to the study of colour in architecture today. Is it because of the perception that colour appears to belong to materials that architects customarily design in black and white, adding colour later? Certainly the Neo-Classical tradition was based upon the natural colours of materials, deriving from mistaken assumptions that the temples of Classical Greece were unadorned with colour. There are indications that colours applied in the form of paint – for whatever reason – were often in imitation of the colours of natural materials. The dichotomy certainly seems to account for many of the insensitive juxtapositions of colour in paint and natural materials that are increasingly common in our environment.

Although we are only beginning to understand the mechanisms of the two ways of seeing, it seems clear that they are not mutually exclusive, and it is likely that many intermediate stages exist. Gibson distinguishes them by location: 'filmy disembodied colours floating in a visual field (compared with) the colours of objective surfaces in a visual world. The former look filmy and insubstantial and appear at an indefinite distance, in contrast with the colours of objects in daylight illumination which appear to be localised on and be part of the surface of the object in question.'[3]

Given that perception is a very selective activity concerned with much more than just appearances it is necessary to examine how our concept of the visual world is formed. While it is clear that we can only survive in a functional environment, there is much disagreement on how these functions are expressed. Buildings, for example, are expected to be much more than forms following function. They are symbols, comforting or otherwise, of the places we live in. This raises the question of how a particular environment is perceived, and, more specifically, how we build up our images of the visual world. The visual process is one of scanning. The eyes move, the head, neck and body move, gathering images like the frames of a (movie) film. The rate of scanning is variable, but generally slow enough to make the illusion of movement in films possible. From these images (and other sensory impressions gathered simultaneously), the scene is constructed together with information already stored in our visual memories, redundant information being filtered out. To what extent cultural and social factors influence this 'editing' process is impossible to assess. In view of the ways in which we exercise taste and discrimination in describing our surroundings, it would appear that the picture of the world on which these judgments are based, is, in many ways, a product of our own imagination.

Learning to see colour

While the precise optical and neurological processes involved in perception are still largely obscure, we know that 'visual awareness' can be learnt. Learning to see – or perhaps more cynically, learning to see with the eyes of our teachers is a prerogative of all courses in art and design education. That there are many different interpretations of this process, at least in its applications, is all too apparent. Of these, colour is one of the most problematical.

The essential connection between colour and objects begins in infancy. As babies we are attracted by the lightness and brightness of things. But it is only later, probably with the beginning of the development of abstract concepts that are facilitated by language, that we learn to perceive colour as a separate sensation; identification is an aid to sight. Observations of a group of children revealed that this was occurring around the age of four and a half. Before then the majority matched objects according to shape rather than colour. But after that age, as culture demands, training in practical skills which rely more heavily on shape than colour the number of choices made according to colour decrease continuously into adulthood. This is perhaps not, in itself, surprising. The important distinction is that the colours of objects in the ordinary sunlit visual world are not the same as the patchwork (of colours) in the corresponding visual field.

Almost all of us have some capacity to sense colour in a detached way. The blue of the sky for example, is essentially filmy and insubstantial like that of the blue haze obscuring distant mountains; also the colours of the rainbow, although revealed by different means, are similarly insubstantial. Most people are aware of the shimmering mirage-like appearance of buildings seen at a distance. Rasmussen compares the view of Manhattan from a ship approaching over 13 miles of water with that of Venice seen across the lagoon, which he describes as 'architecture experienced as colour-planes'.[4] Such effects are typically expressed by the indistinct patches of colour in paintings by Nicholas de Stael (1914-1955). There are close parallels also in the 'dazzle-painting' effects of camouflage on ships during the First World War which made them appear to be steaming in different directions and some recent uses of the technique to disguise, or reduce the bulking effect of some buildings.

Another quite common effect is that in which natural light is seen to transform the visual world from its everyday appearance to one of light and colour. It occurs at its most impressive when the sun is low and the sky is dark with storm clouds. As the sun moves towards the horizon, more and more of the short blue wavelengths are absorbed by the atmosphere, which transmit mainly long ones. The intense red and yellow light turns everything to gold, transforming all objects. All colours: greens, reds, browns and greys, are united in the harmony of a single dominant hue, contrasting with the dark blue-grey of the sky.[5] The two 'modes of seeing' have been described by RH Thouless in 1931 as 'the object mode' and the 'illuminant mode'. The former refers to the everyday world in which we all live; which so often seems devoid of light and colour, that we seek compensation in artificial lighting effects and an extravagant use of applied colour.

Colour and light

Painters have always acknowledged the problem of painting light, but as an aspect of objects or their backgrounds. For Turner, after about 1820, luminosity and atmosphere began to predominate in his paintings, until, in the last years of his life, pictorial subjects seemed to dissolve in light and colour. Although rooted in the Romantic tradition of ideal landscapes peopled with images from antiquity, depicted in sombre melancholy colours, he

FROM ABOVE: Bruno Taut , Weissensee housing project, Berlin; Bruno Taut, Hufeisensiedlung housing project, Berlin; Waldsiedlung Zehlendorf (Onkel Tom's Hütte), Berlin

progressed towards a fresh and original view of nature and natural forces, not copied, but expressed by natural harmonies of colour. His palette changed to one of clear brilliant colours, anticipating many of the prescriptions of Goethe's *Theory of Colours*, which only came into his hands in translation in 1843.

Like Turner, Monet devoted the latter part of his life to portraying the atmosphere of colour. Figures almost disappear from his paintings. He stopped travelling and began to concentrate on a series of paintings of individual subjects: haystacks, poplars, Rouen Cathedral and the Gare St Lazare. The rural subjects are lacking in topographical interest and the paintings of buildings tell us little about the architecture. He had become absorbed, as Turner had more than half a century before, in the changing effects of light and colour to such an extent that the subject had ceased to be important; 'For me a landscape does not exist in its own right, since its appearance changes at every moment; but the surrounding atmosphere brings it to life – the air and the light which vary continually. For me, it is only the surrounding atmosphere which gives subjects their true value.'[6] He draws attention to the apparent difference in scale between buildings seen in direct sunlight with shadows, and seen in diffused light; an important distinction for those selecting colours for buildings.

Turner had worked mostly in isolation and developed his own theory of colours. The Impressionists – a loose association of avant-garde artists – had the benefits both of common interests and scientific and industrial backing. Industrial production included the synthesization and production of colours, the development of optics, photography, colour printing, and it included the development of colour theories. Of the latter, the volume by ME Chevreul entitled, *The Principles of Harmony and Contrast of Colours*, was outstanding for three main reasons; first, it was practical, setting out the uses of colour in every imaginable field from textiles to painting and from architecture to horticulture; second, it dealt sensibly with the subject of colour harmonies; and third, it provided explanations for such peculiarities as optical mixing and simultaneous contrast. Chevreul's explanation that orange sunlight produced violet shadows offered invaluable guidance to the Impressionist painters, providing an argument against those who were suspicious of the sensory approach to colour.

Colour expression

Turner and Monet had explored the atmosphere of light and colour in nature, the Expressionists turned away from the representation of nature as a primary purpose of art, towards the direct expression of feelings and emotions through line, form and colour. In 1908, Matisse wrote; 'What I am after, above all, is expression . . . The chief aim of colour should be to serve expression as well as possible . . . To paint an autumn landscape I will try to remember what colour suits the season; I will be inspired only by the sensation the season gives me'.[7]

Expressionist groups had appeared almost simultaneously in France and Germany, les Fauves having combined in their art the theories of Van Gogh and Gauguin and retained a certain harmony of design; die Brücke used form and colour to express drama and violence. 'We accept all the colours, which, directly or indirectly, reproduce the pure creative impulse.'[8]

This was no longer the atmospheric colour of Turner and Monet, but strong, highly-saturated colour imbued with meaning; and, as with most German art, the meaning was weighted with philosophical concepts. The process by which colours and forms themselves became the repositories of the pictorial ideas was carried to its

logical conclusion in abstraction. Attempts to reconcile the more anarchic impulses of Expressionism with the need for social reform were realised in the ideas of the activist movement, in particular, in the architecture of Bruno Taut (1880-1938), and in the principles on which the Bauhaus (1919-1933) was founded.

The importance of colour at the Bauhaus was ensured by the appointment of many artists and designers who had been connected with the Expressionist movement in painting; the links with form and space were confirmed by the foundation course, Colour and Form, taught by Johannes Itten, Paul Klee and Wassily Kandinsky. Each had a different approach, which become clear with the subsequent development. Itten and Kandinsky believed in a correlation between emotional states, colours and forms. The latter had derived his colour theory from Goethe via the anthroposophist Rudolf Steiner, and had published a paper in 1912 entitled, *Concerning the Spiritual in Art*. From an early age he had experienced synaesthesia (the association of colour with music), wanting colours to exist purely for their own sake, as sounds do. Klee, an accomplished violinist, considered that the pitch of colours functioned like major or minor keys, enabling a person to 'improvise freely on the chromatic keyboard'.[9] Characteristically, drawing for Klee was like 'a line going for a walk', changing its character according to what happened on the way, but he saw colour as the richest aspect of optical experience. While line is only measurement, tone is measurement and weight and colour is quality.

The building as art

Although the influence of the Bauhaus has been profound in all areas of design, it did not immediately stimulate the use of applied colour to the outsides of buildings. White was and remains in the common perception, the colour of the Modern Movement, as it had been the colour of Neo-Classicism. Apart from the elaborate and extensive uses in the social projects of Bruno Taut, applied colour was limited to a few individual buildings. Gerrit Rietveld's recently restored Schröder-Schräder house in Utrecht is a work of art. The purity of line and surface speak of a time when painters, sculptors and architects could work together to such an extent that their work seems interchangeable. With remarkable restraint strong saturated colours have been restricted to linear and structural elements – a lesson that might have been learnt from nature. Volumes resolve themselves into subtly coloured advancing and receding planes which seduce the eye with the elegance of their proportions: all of which reminds one that De Stijl is so much more suited to buildings than to chairs.

Le Corbusier's Pessac houses would seem also to have fitted the category of 'building as art'. Saying that he wanted to do something poetic, Corbusier chose a painter's approach. He embraced colour completely, seeking to achieve an effect of weightlessness by painting the surfaces in different colours which met at the corners, so that a light grey, for example, bordered on a light sky-blue without any hint of structural thickness. Rasmussen describes his experience of sitting in the shade of a maple tree in the roof garden of one of the houses;

> I could see how the sun dappled the Havana-brown wall with blobs of light. The only purpose of the wall was to frame the view. The buildings opposite could be perceived as houses only with great difficulty. The one to the left was simply a light-green plane without cornice or gutter. An oblong hole was cut out of the plane exactly like the one I was looking through. Behind and to the right of the green house were row houses

with coffee-brown facades and cream-coloured sides and behind them rose the tops of blue . . . [10]

Colour and social housing

Bruno Taut was also torn between painting and architecture. In his diary he wrote;

thoughts about painting occupy me constantly. It seems to me that I can give my character its fullest expression in this medium . . . The idea . . . (of a) combination of my talents with regard to colour with my architectural ability. Spatial composition with colour, coloured architecture – these are areas in which I shall perhaps say something special . . . [11]

The opportunity to combine the rational and social skills of the architect with the vision of a painter came in 1914, when he was commissioned to design the small garden suburb of Falkenberg, near Grünau, in east Berlin. The colours selected were light red, dull olive-green, golden-brown, strong (saturated) blue, and white. Some contemporary observers interpreted the use of colours as a form of liberation, freeing working-men's housing from the tyranny of refined and alien forms. Taut saw it as a means of 'liberating German architecture from the strait-jacket of muddy grey styles.'[12]

When he won a place on the Board of Works of the industrial city of Magdeburg in March 1921, Taut immediately announced his intention to transform the city, 'tired of being regarded as a mere suburb of Berlin'. Unbroken colour (unmodified strong colour), he considered, was what the city needed, and Breiter Weg, the main business thoroughfare, was selected for the first phase. Although he succeeded in this and in having a number of public buildings painted, as a public experiment it was a failure. The air was too dirty, the cement render crumbled and the paint was of poor quality. The result, after little less than a year, was disastrous, and he resigned.

As artistic director of the planning division of GEHAG, Bruno Taut had more freedom to implement his ideas of colour without the need for public cooperation. With foreign capital supporting the building industry a number of estates was built throughout the city. These included a line of low-cost slab blocks of flats, in Prenslauer Berg in the district of Weissensee. They were boldly painted with broad bands of red and blue against white – an interesting early solution to the problem of giving identity to mass- and high-rise housing by means of colour. The two other main coloured developments were the Hufeisensiedlung (named after the horseshoe shaped central block) and the Waldsiedlung Zehlendorf (Onkel Tom's Hütte).

In the last of the five phases of the Waldsiedlung Zehlendorf the building authorities required a unified colour scheme to be submitted in advance for approval. The five parallel streets of off-set two-storey houses were painted in Pompeian red and bluish green, alternating left and right, with the complementary scheme being reversed on the backs of the houses. The facades were articulated with bands of glazed brick in the Mondrian manner and dividing walls of natural red brick; and the window, frames and doors carefully articulated in black and white, red and yellow. The use of the complementary red and green reflected the conditions of natural lighting: the east-facing facades being green, and the west-facing walls red. The colours of window frames were keyed in to the particular background wall colour in each case; and the ends of the streets were 'closed' with strategically coloured blocks. Taut described the colour choices in terms of space;

colour should be used to underline the spatial character of the development. By means of variation in colour intensity and brilliance we can expand the space between the house rows in certain directions and compress it in others.[13]

The fact that applied colour has survived on the houses of all these estates is a measure of Taut's success. It has degenerated in the sense that weather has washed and bleached the paints and changes have been made. But this degeneration can be seen also as an aspect of human evolution, particularly now that restorations have been undertaken. It is becoming clear that, in addition to the planning framework for the use of colour, some degree of flexibility is desirable. But the message is clear, as Taut wrote in 1925;

Everything in the world has colour of some sort. Nature has colour, even the grey of dust and soot, even gloom has colour of some kind. Where there is light, there must be colour. All man has to do is to give this phenomenon form . . . [14]

With the rise of National Socialism, as opposed to Taut's own version of Socialism, his work came to an end, and he took an appointment in Turkey. The Bauhaus was forced to close in 1933, and many of its teachers left for America; and there were serious suggestions that the flat-roofed buildings of the Weissenhofsiedlung – regarded as symbolic of degenerate eastern Mediterranean architecture – should have pitched roofs added.

Michael Lancaster is an architect and landscape architect. He has written Colourscape, *to be published by Academy Editions in 1996 and* Britain in View: Colour and the Landscape, *the subject of a BBC2 film series,* The Colour Eye.

Notes

1 Roy Osborne, *Lights and Pigments*, (Edwin Land quoted), John Murray Publishers (London), 1981.

2 Bomford, Kirby, Leighton, Roy, *Impressionism*, National Gallery and Yale University Press (London), 1990.

3 J J Gibson, *Perception of the Visual World*, Greenwood (Connecticut), 1977.

4 S E Rasmussen, *Experiencing Architecture*, MIT Press (Cambridge), 1959.

5 Michael Lancaster, *Britain in View: Colour and the Landscape*, Quiller Press (London), 1984.

6 J House, *Monet*, Phaidon (Oxford), 1981.

7 Harold Osborne ed, *Oxford Companion to Art*, Oxford University Press (Oxford), 1971-81 (Henri Matisse quoted 1908).

8 Harold Osborne (ed), *Oxford Companion to Art*, (Ludwig Kirchner quoted 1913).

9 Hope and Walch, *The Colour Compendium*, Van Nostrum Reinhold (New York), 1990.

10 S E Rasmussen, *Experiencing Architecture*, MIT Press (Cambridge), 1959.

11 B Whyte, *Architecture of Activism*, Cambridge University Press (Cambridge).

12 Düttmann, Schmuck, Uhl, *Color in Townscape*, Architectural Press (London), 1981.

13 Ibid.

14 Bruno Taut, Rebirth of Colour, 1925 lecture (quoted in Düttmann, Schmuck, Uhl, *Color in Townscape*).

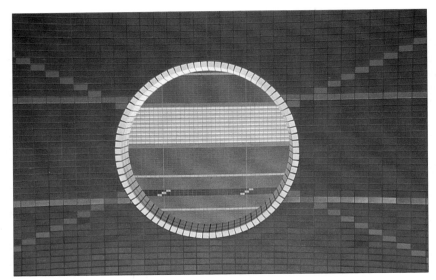

LEFT, FROM ABOVE: Pacific Design Centre, West Hollywood, California, 1988; Sea Hawk Hotel and Resort, Fukuoka, Japan, 1995; California Jewellery Mart, Los Angeles, California, 1968; RIGHT, FROM ABOVE: Pacific Design Centre, Sea Hawk Hotel and Resort

CESAR PELLI
DESIGNING WITH COLOUR

When I was asked to write an article on colour in architecture my first thought was that all materials have colour. Some are muted and some bright. Whites, greys and browns are colours as well as reds and yellows. The question is, what colours to use in each circumstance? I am also aware that by colour in architecture we normally mean colours as architectural elements in themselves, not only as definers of form. We also mean the use of saturated colours, contrasting colours, or colour used as a decorative element.

The use of bright, contrasting or decorative colours result from two traditions: one is an ancient tradition in many cultures of using only natural materials for the exterior of buildings – they tend to be mostly shades of grey and brown or stone and wood. Of course, there have been exceptions; red or orange brick buildings that were not seen as coloured because of local consistency. The same was true of the deep ochre of Tuscany. Some buildings were brightly coloured to mark them as exceptions, such as the vermilion shrines in Japan. The other tradition is that of Modernism which perceived architecture primarily as white, black or grey, with primary colours used only as accents.

I am primarily a designer–builder and not an academic scholar, and I believe that I can best explain my thoughts on this matter in terms of my experiences and through some of my projects.

When I was a student of architecture in Tucumán, Argentina, I learned that proper, serious Modern architecture should have no colour except for the colours of natural materials, whites or greys – anything else was frivolous or decadent. In the years after the Second World War, students of architecture in progressive schools all over the world must have learned the same lessons. There were several reasons for the avoidance of colour in Modernism: one was the opposition to the highly decorated eclectic architecture that Modernism was trying to replace; another was the personal preference of the main shaper of Modern architecture – Le Corbusier and his work as a Purist painter. In orthodox Modernism there was also a desire to go back to basics, to strip down architecture to its essentials in an ethical and formal cleansing. Perhaps the most pervasive reason was that orthodox Modernists believed in the imminent triumph of science, technology and reason and tried to base their architecture on rational design. Strong colours must have been seen as appealing directly to the senses, bypassing the prescribed filter of reason.

I started my career in architecture as an apprentice to Eero Saarinen. Saarinen used colour as a Modernist; his architecture took the colour of natural materials, or was finished in whites, greys and blacks with occasional bright coloured accents such as the glazed brick walls of the General Motors Technical Centre.

When I started practising on my own, although within larger firms such as DMJM and Gruen, I did not feel constrained by Modernist strictures although I was, and still consider myself to be, a Modern architect. One of the first projects I had at DMJM was the remodelling of an old office building on the corner of

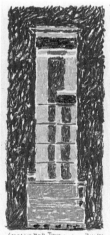

ABOVE: Sketch of Herring Hall, Rice University, Houston, Texas, 1984; CENTRE LEFT: Sketch of Sea Hawk Hotel and Resort, Fukuoka, Japan, 1995; CENTRE RIGHT: Sketch of Carnegie Hall Tower, New York, 1991; BELOW: Sketch of Pacific Design Centre, West Hollywood, California, 1988

Museum of Modern Art (MoMA) expansion and renovation sketches, New York, 1984

Pershing Square in Los Angeles that was being transformed into a jewellery mart. I had an extremely small budget. The areas for re-design were a lobby, where all I did was to clean it up, and a deep courtyard – nine storeys deep. To renovate the courtyard I was given a total construction budget of $16,000 which meant that I could afford little else besides paint. I designed a simple but strong pattern that transformed the dingy and unpleasant space into one that was bright and lively and a pleasure to look at. The forms were abstract and very much in tune with modern currents in the visual arts; therefore, I felt that I was only slightly stretching the artistic envelope of Modernism. This was my first built design to be recognised on the cover of an architectural magazine (*Progressive Architecture*, February 1968).

The Pacific Design Centre is a more instructive example, the form is simple, abstract and certainly Modern. By cladding the large building in bright blue ceramic glass I gave it a new quality, a direct impact to our senses. To me this meant adding another perceptual dimension to the artistic possibilities of architecture. There was something else of perhaps greater importance – if the building had been grey or brown (such as my earlier design for the San Bernadino City Hall) it would not have had the ability to engage the lay passer-by as completely as the Pacific Design Centre did. The building quickly gained an affectionate nickname, the Blue Whale. The colour established an emotional link between object and observer that is absent in many of the abstract colourless compositions we architects admire but are not understood or appreciated by the public at large. Some years later I had the opportunity to design an addition to the Pacific Design Centre, that appeared as a large, green sculptural form. The large-scale ensemble of coloured forms created an even more accessible and appreciated architecture, which was very rewarding for me.

A few years after the design of the Pacific Design Centre, I was commissioned to design the major renovation and expansion of the Museum of Modern Art in New York which included the design of a residential tower built on top of the museum addition. I was able to experiment with the use of colour for a more complex artistic purpose just as I had with two apartment buildings I designed in Houston (Four Leaf Towers) at approximately the same time. Glass towers have often been used to house office space, their abstract uniform nature can be justified because they enclose undifferentiated modular space for undetermined users –

every window on every floor is the same as any other. However, the MoMA Tower was a residential building with predetermined functions and it was important to express this character on its exterior and to express the changing sizes and relationships among living rooms, bedrooms and other functions. My design for MoMA started with saturated colours but I had to tone them down several times to have them approved. The building is now elegant, but not exuberant.

My work in ceramic glass progressed from the rational and somehow didactic gridded enclosure I designed for the San Bernardo City Hall to the addition of colour to a similarly gridded volume in the Pacific Design Centre, giving a new sensorial dimension to the MoMA and Four Leaf Towers. In these buildings the gridded glass wall became less abstract and more expressive of the functions it enclosed. This was not an issue of colour, but colour was the vehicle available to me. These designs represented my growing belief in the need for Modern architecture to evolve from a dogmatic and narrow position towards an architecture with a wider range of expressions capable of answering all of society's needs.

Herring Hall at Rice University, represented for me a further and critical elaboration of this line of thought. Herring Hall houses the school of business at Rice University. This is a small, beautiful and coherent campus designed by Ralph Adams Cram of the firm, Cram Goodhue and Ferguson of Boston, and by his disciple, William Ward Watkins, in the first and second decades of this century. The character of the Cram-Watkins buildings is romantic, colourful and very appropriate to its functions and to the climate of Houston. It was also based on materials and craftsmanship that were no longer affordable. The problem for Cesar Pelli & Associates was one of designing a suitable building to become part of an ensemble of buildings that I respected but could not imitate for intellectual and economical reasons. I resolved this dilemma by designing a contemporary building with colours and details of similar density to those of Cram. The basic colour is a salmon brick, with accents of limestone and glazed bricks and tiles. The sense of colour is achieved more by the juxtaposition of materials than by the use of highly saturated pigments. The lessons learned in Herring Hall gave me the tools with which to design the office tower for Carnegie Hall, a problem that would have been otherwise unmanageable.

One of my latest experiments in using colour on a building to

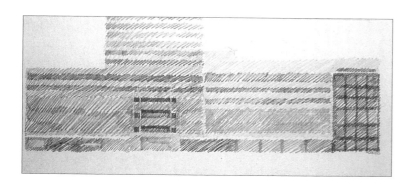

heighten its expressive and artistic qualities was in the Sea Hawk Resort Hotel that was recently built on Hakata Bay in the city of Fukuoka. The complex functions of a resort hotel require volumes of different dimensions and characteristics. I took advantage of the availability in Japan of beautiful and economical ceramic tiles and of a skilled work force well trained in their application. I developed the skin of ceramic tile as a critical element that gives character to the building, a character appropriate to a seaside resort hotel. The use of colours and patterns in this building allowed me to express, as I have in all the previous ones, the nature of contemporary buildings: air-conditioned spaces enclosed by thin, lightweight walls. These walls are two-dimensional surfaces defining three-dimensional hollow volumes. The patterns have a character-giving role and they also create what I call a 'supersurface' that guides our eyes across voids and around corners, strengthening the taut qualities of the building's envelope.

Colour in architecture is quite unlike that in painting; first of all it is colour in three dimensions. It is also subjected to changing sunlight and, most importantly, it requires the careful use of materials with necessary consideration to their ageing and weathering properties. Wood will grey and darken with age, copper will start its life as golden, turn dark brown, and in fifteen to twenty years will become bright green. Stone will grey and may acquire a green patina of moss. Ceramic materials in glass or glazed bricks and tiles will maintain their colour relatively unchanged through the years. Paint fades rapidly under sunlight and brightly painted coloured walls need repainting every three years or so. These considerations are essential to the craft and art of architecture. To produce good architecture, intuition is essential but is not enough, it also requires considerable doses of rational thought. It is this interplay of reason and intuition that I find most satisfying and often exhilarating in the practice of my art.

I have to qualify my enthusiasm for the use of colours in my designs. We must always bear in mind that sometimes colours are appropriate and sometimes they are not, it depends on the context. In a town or neighbourhood of buildings coloured only by natural materials a brightly coloured structure (or white or black) could do great harm to the total ensemble, and I believe the whole is always more important than one of its parts even if that part happens to be one of my buildings.

FROM ABOVE: Four Leaf Towers, Houston, Texas, 1992; Sea Hawk Hotel and Resort, Fukuoka, Japan, 1995

TOMÁS TAVEIRA

GENERAL ASSEMBLY BUILDING EXTENSION
Lisbon, Portugal

The General Assembly extension is designed to supply office space, conference rooms and a public space. It is located beside an established older building and below the gardens of the prime minister's official house in Lisbon.

In addition to his architectural work for banks and government buildings, Taveira has moved into mass media, designing sets for both stage and television. This popularity and acute awareness of the need for diversity is typical of Taveira's thought and constant flux. He can also subdue his humour for the 'serious' National Assembly Palace in Lisbon while also subverting established associations with buildings such as the Penitentiary in Dordrecht, which mirrors the attempts of the Dutch to radically alter the idea of imprisonment.

Taveira's overriding concern for building into a specific context – his particular and personal context of Lisbon – has led him to the use of colour, which strikes chords, resonates in the hearts and minds of the Lisbon people and taps, so it seems, the 'collective unconscious'.

Taveira's diverse career includes his early concrete-prefabricated social housing in the periphery of Lisbon and his gradual rejection of 'puritanism', embracing colour and diversity.

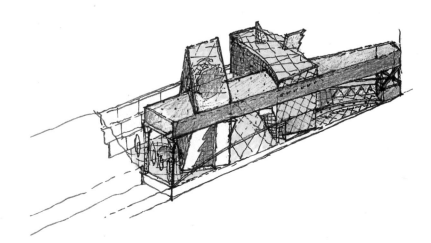

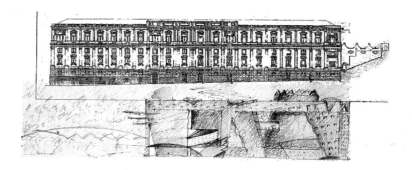

OPPOSITE: Computer generated images of exterior perspectives; FROM ABOVE: Sketch designs

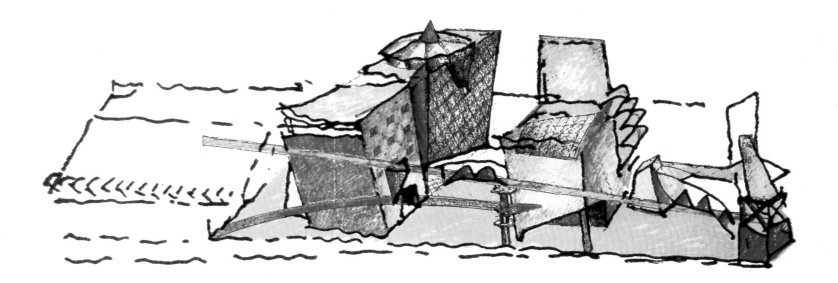

LEGORRETA ARCHITECTS
SAN ANTONIO LIBRARY
San Antonio, Texas

The City of San Antonio wanted a joyful building, far removed from the stuffy image of ordinary library facilities, a building the community would celebrate as its own, and a building that housed state-of-the-art technology for information access. In a traditional sense, the challenge of this project was to achieve a well developed architectural language which integrates the library functions and uses.

Described by local critics as an 'ingenious blending of design and function', the new facility can be compared with the old on only one level: both are places where books are kept. Books remain a critical element in the new facility, but it shows an appreciation for the other important elements in San Antonio's library facility: architecture, art and technology.

The capacity of the library has been doubled to 22,300 square metres, with space for up to 750,000 books.

The building's geometry of rotated, cut-away boxes, largely determined by the spatial restrictions of the site, allows people to view the library as a friendly, accessible and inviting building.

The exterior 'is a visual wonderland of shapes, angles, and openings that create an interplay of light and shadows, both inside and outside the building'.

The area is distributed on seven storeys, six of them above ground. The main mass is a six-storey box surrounding a yellow skylit atrium that serves as a focal point for each floor. Some terraces are accented by large geometric shapes. Triangular and rectangular baffle walls painted purple or yellow on the third floor terraces generate curiosity and invite people to go outside. Another terrace to the west is bordered by a slightly raised *acequia,* a water channel, that pours into a circular pool. Beyond the *acequia* stands a grove of palm trees. Exterior walls are finished with acrylic plaster. At street level, a stone wainscot gives scale to the building.

Blending natural light, shadow and geometric figures throughout the new library, creates a sense of mystery. Visitors discover something new at each visit, to entice them back, time after time.

The design evokes a sense of freedom, particularly in the use of space. This is accomplished by giving the library floors unique personalities by varying their shape and size. The differences encourage visitors to discover the building in all its variety.

Special features for children have been incorporated into the design of the third floor. Architectural elements and graduated child-size stacks, scaled-down furnishings and abundant natural light put young people at ease in an environment tailored to their needs.

Designed to incorporate many future innovations, the library's new card catalogue is on the cutting edge of computing technology; including a kid's card catalogue, a Spanish card catalogue, Internet access and a search system that allows access to libraries across the USA.

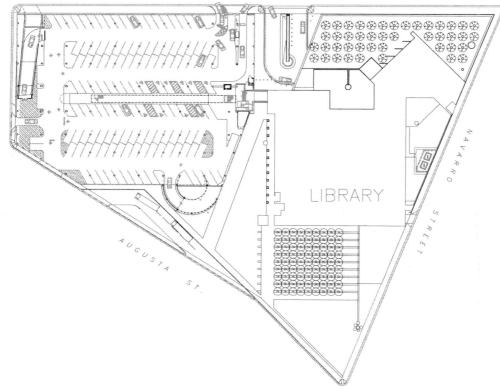

LIBRARY

Site plan

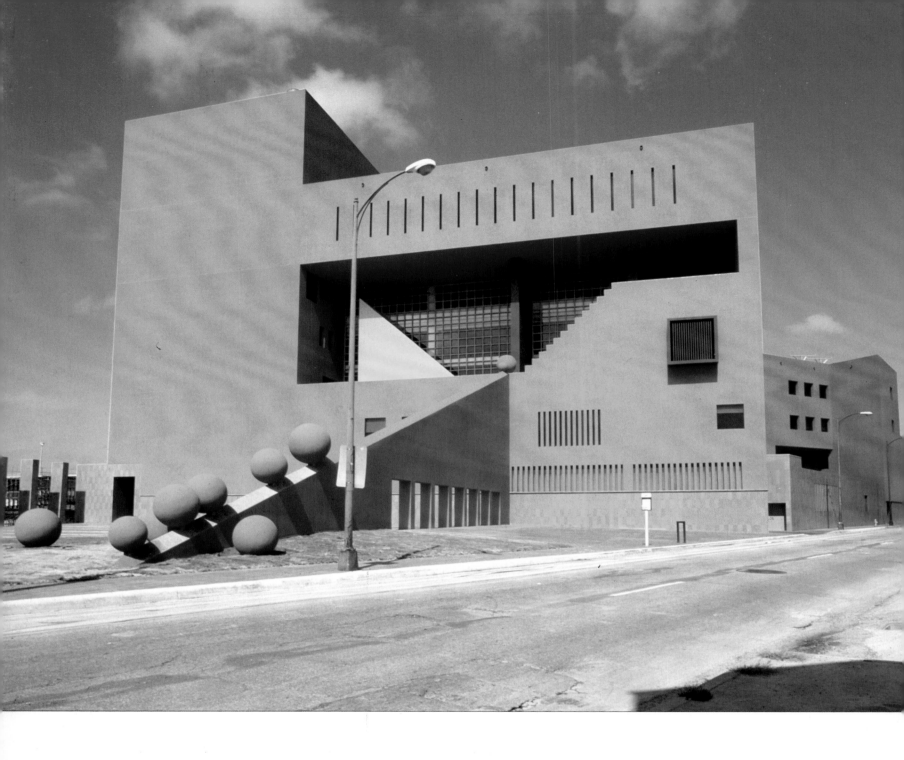

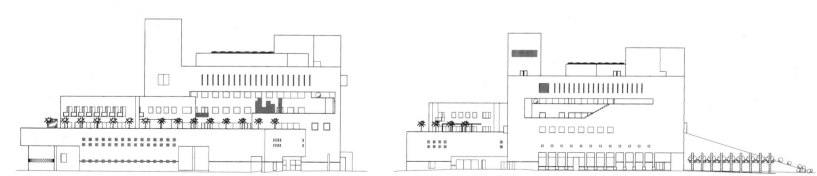

West elevation; south elevation

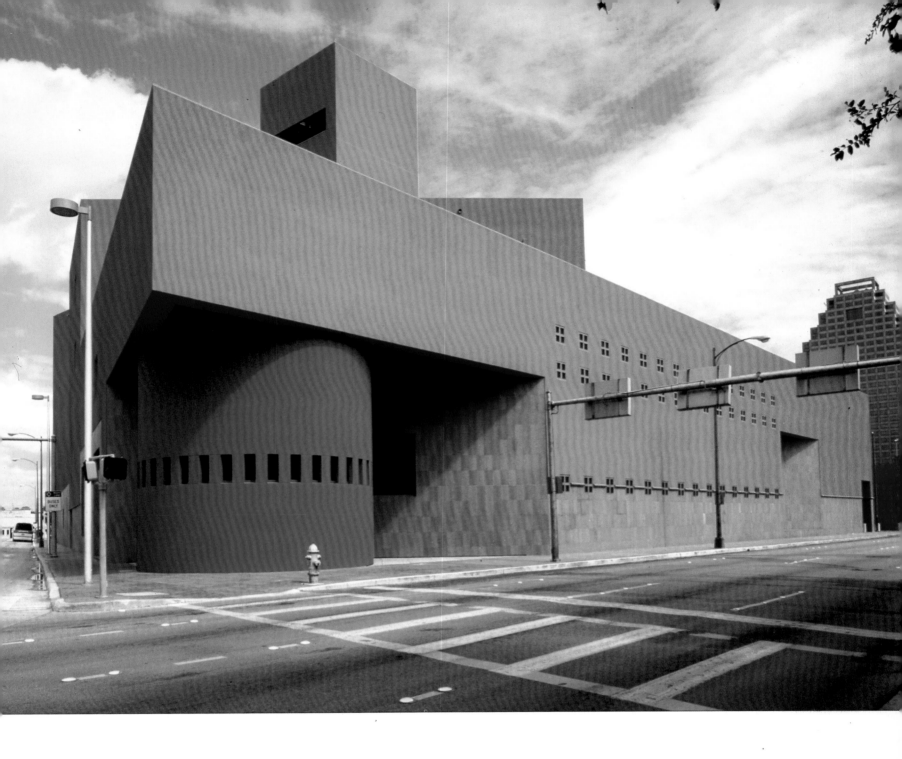

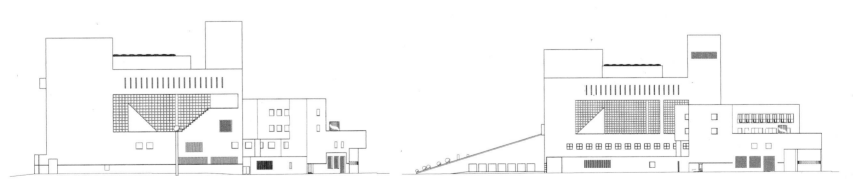

East elevation; north elevation

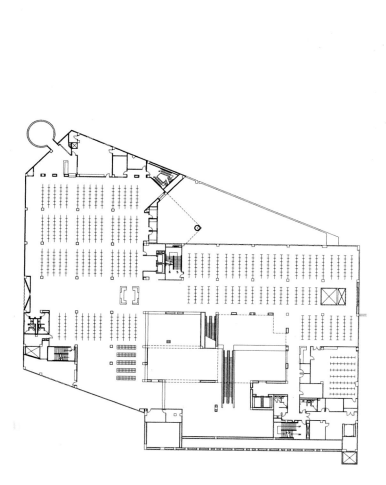

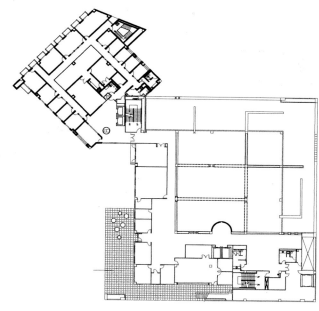

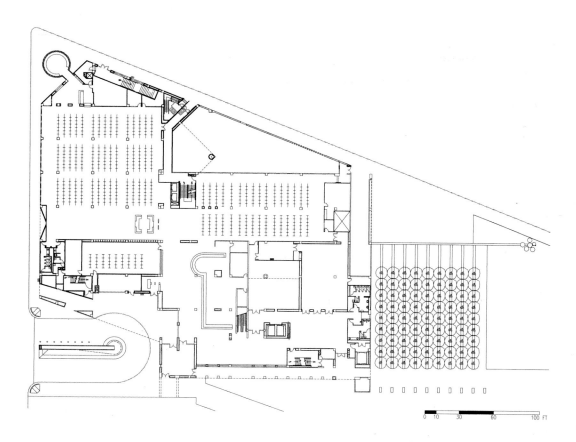

FROM ABOVE: Fourth floor plan;
second floor plan; ground floor plan

0 10   30   50   100 FT

SOLANA
Dallas, Texas

Solana, the 'sunny place', is a 900-acre business community just 10 minutes west of DFW International Airport in Dallas, Fort Worth. A team of three architectural firms, Mitchel Giurgola, Barton Mayers and Legorreta Architects along with landscape architect, Peter Walker, developed a simple scheme that took advantage of the highway that crossed the property. As a result, an underpass was designed to form part of the master plan. When complete in the late 1990s, it will encompass some seven million square feet of office space in a self-contained business community.

Unity was set by the interplay on walls, height, scale, materials and colour. Each architect was free to design and express his style, respecting simple guidelines, this allowed for a dialogue between the buildings.

The master plan preserves the natural beauty of the site's wild flower fields, prairie grasslands, and oak groves. It combines a low density, campus-style environment with the character of the southwest. Growth will be carefully controlled to ensure the quality of the environment long-term.

Solana contains two main office spaces: Seven Village Circle and Nine Village Circle. These two buildings provide 300,000 square feet of office space. The distinctive architecture and exceptional interiors of these two five-storey buildings blend limestone, stucco, clear glass, and vibrant colours with porticoed entrances, arcades, interior atriums and outdoor balconies.

Vertical elements were created as directional entry symbols. The use of walls, plazas, textures and colour, contributed to create intimate spaces but, at the same time, humanise the almost unlimited scale of the Texas landscape.

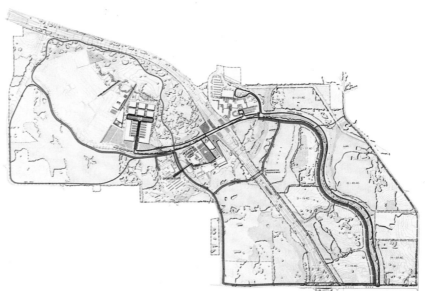

Master site plan

Village site plan

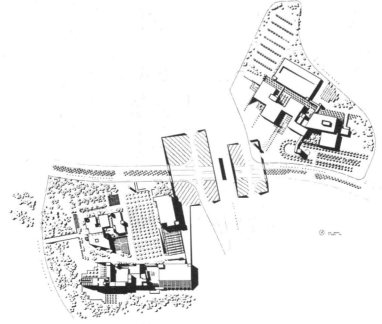

HENRI CIRIANI

MUSEUM OF ANCIENT ARLES
Arles, France

The concept of the museum has in effect only emerged in the last 80 years, although it has now developed to a much-heralded status. Hollein's project at Mönchengladbach, Meier's in Frankfurt, Pei's in Washington and Stirling's in Stuttgart opens the way for reflection on the edifice for which anterior references barely exist. The Museum of Ancient Arles was built to deal with the existing and increasing amount of Roman artefacts from the surrounding area in Southern France and set up sophisticated excavation projects and research groups.

The museum was to bring a new aspect of history to the town. Surrounded by water – the Rhone to the west, the Midi Canal to the east – this near-island, set on a triangle of land, is immediately imposing. Far removed from all things Roman, the triangular form responds, however, to the perfect oval of the amphitheatre of the old town, echoing the brutal geometries of the configurations of the new town. From a geographical point of view, the island harmonises with the urban context.

The triangle responds perfectly to the design which demanded both a short and a long route. The design is integrated logically in this form, with three sections: the scientific (catering operations, temporary exhibitions and stock, in addition to the school of excavation); the cultural (where teaching takes place, the library, conference room, administration, and foyer) and finally, the school for museum guides. These elements constitute two buildings which between them contain the museum proper.

The main facade is perpendicular to the sluice gate of the Midi canal, which enables the building to be anchored to an artificial element. This first wall, facing onto the old town, is not well-developed. It is the original element of the project as well as the facade of the immense juxtaposing circle in which the excavations are taking place. Behind lies the cultural wing, a white building, set against the

heart of the city. The second facade looks onto the canal and dominates the scientific wing which is oriented towards the point of the near-island. This area, facing the Rhone, introduces the museum with its extension facing the town.

In the centre, the patio contains a grand staircase which is incorporated into the roof detail, thus completing the museographic route. This element fills the central void, giving direction to the helix while at the same time rendering it complete. The roof comprises the fourth facade of the building, as important as the three others and revealing in terms of internal organisation on account of the skyward lighting system.

The architecture as a whole is very dependent on the quality of light. A group of open shed-roofs to the north directs the light from the perimeter of the facade. This type of lighting, borrowed from the industrial world, has endowed the museum with architectural ingenuity. Here waves of white homogenous light seem to ripple, escaping to the ceiling. Another type of light is obtained by brackets which capture the sunlight and give it a more textured colour. Finally, the so-called 'view' lighting enters through openings framed by the countryside.

The blue building panels give this light a somewhat cold quality. This material and this colour were already present in the most ancient projects (notably that of the Opera-Bastille) where they conformed with a precise syntax (blue for the contextual elements, red for the functional areas). In Arles, the blue colour refers more simply to the intense colour of the provincial sky.

Since the time of the competition in 1983-84, the evolution of the design has confirmed the pertinence of the triangular form. What was the Museum of Ancient Arles has now become the Institute of Research for Ancient Provence. The museum has expanded from 6,000 to 7,400 square metres without detracting from the initial concept.

BELOW: Cross-section; north-west section, north-east section

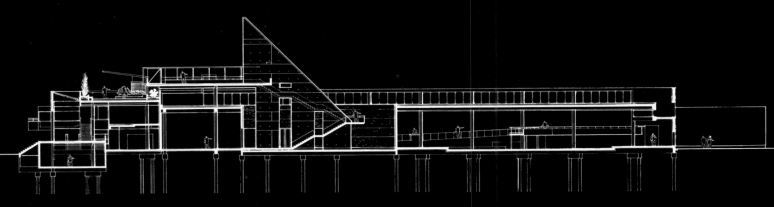

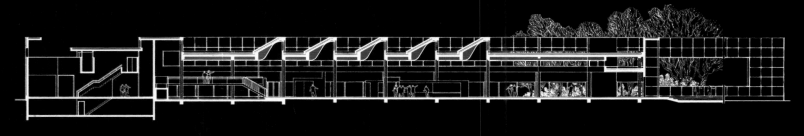

Axonometric

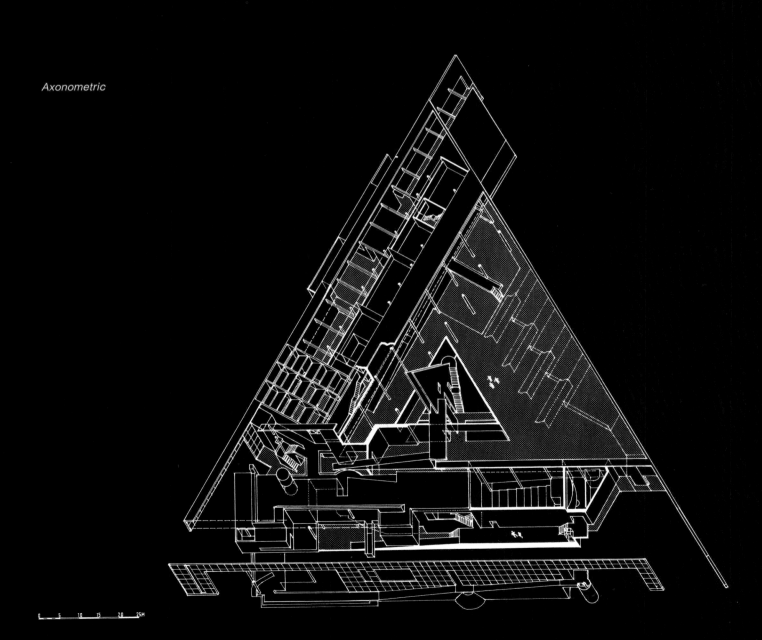

0 5 10 15 20 25M

47

VOETS ARCHITECTS
DELTA SCHOOL
Delft, The Netherlands

The limited site area allowed little scope for an extensive spatial programme which was to include eight classrooms and a kindergarten. After consulting the urban design department of the municipality they agreed to set the building partly in an existing polder ditch.

The reflections in the surface of the water, the colours and the form of the structure itself lend the school complex an individuality and distinctiveness that set it off from the provisional school building nearby.

The layout is based on a linear circulation spine to which classroom units and other rooms are informally attached on both sides. The resulting ensemble of small blocks with projections and indentations contains an element of surprise and adventure. At the same time, the flat roofs over all parts of the school give this cubic structure the order and cohesion it requires. The north facade, overlooking the canal, is designed as a transparent front affording an uninterrupted view of the water. This creates a sense of continuity from inside to outside. Along the south facade, garden areas form the transition between the classrooms and the playground. A second, more secluded playground has been laid out on the roof of two single-storey classrooms. Two further classrooms can be added here at a later date as the need arises. To create a better relationship between the two floors there is a spacious void with a connecting steel staircase. From this first floor there is a spectacular view of the Dutch landscape.

The independence of the small blocks is accentuated by the different coloured tiles. The different colours for each individual section stimulate a greater sense of identity on the part of pupils with their own particular classroom.

49

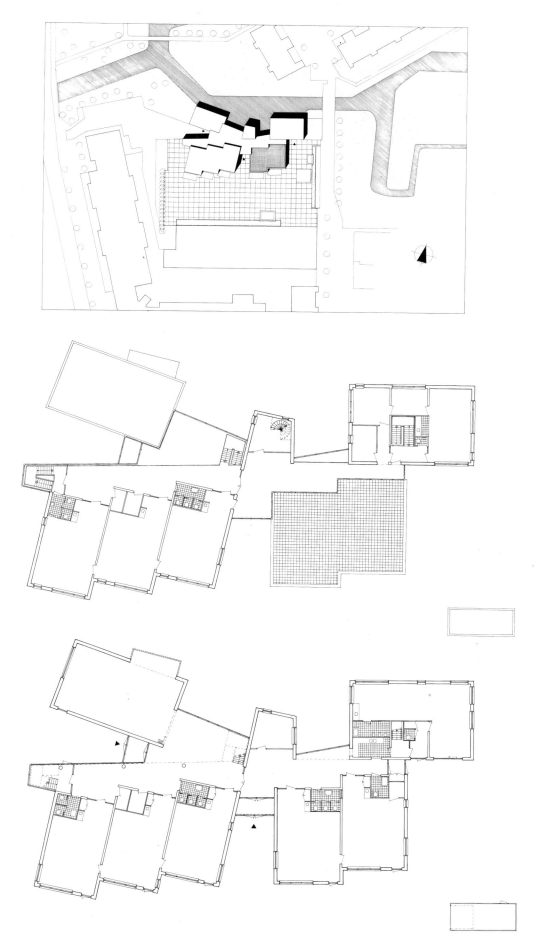

*FROM ABOVE: Site plan; upper floor plan;
ground floor plan*

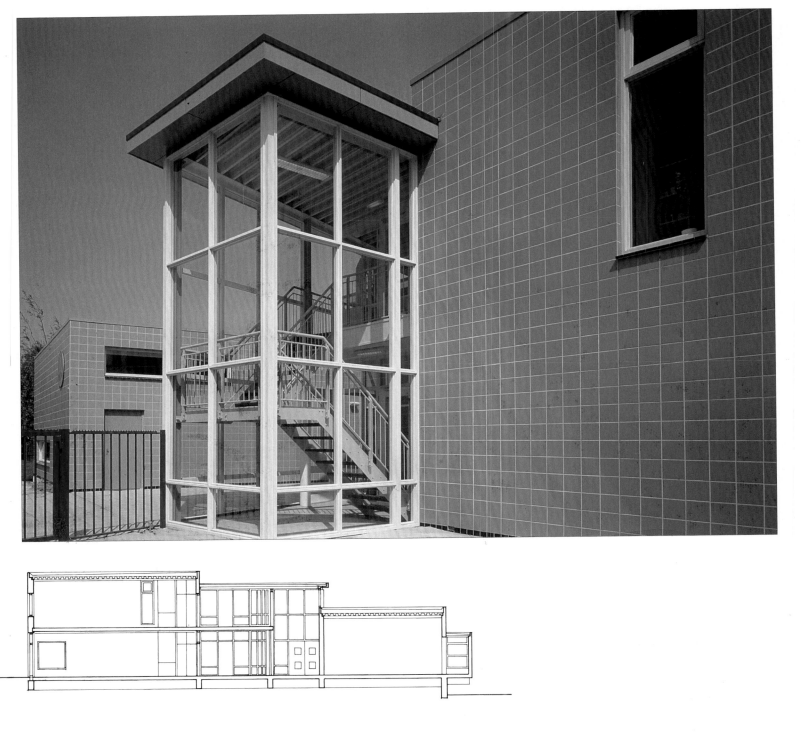

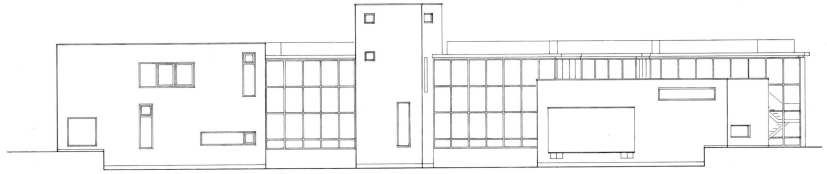

Section; north elevation

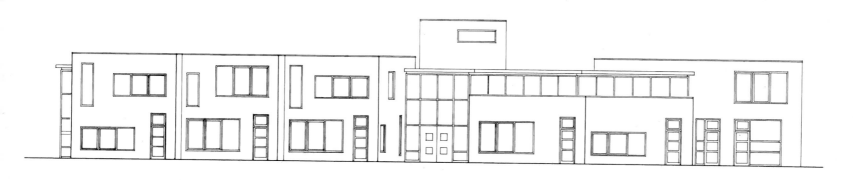

South elevation

ORTNER AND ORTNER ARCHITECTS

MAXX HOTEL

Linz, Austria

Situated spectacularly on the bank of the Danube, the bright colours of the Maxx Hotel stand out against the river. Specific characteristics of the site – including an existing and fully functioning furniture store – resulted in the formation of two wings, one rather oblique and somewhat asymmetrical, around a central space. The splayed construction of the side wing allows extra light and space into the interior.

The dramatic colouring of the building (one section is yellow, the other red) imitates a certain Italianate styling, and acquires a Mediterranean feel. Large slabs in the inner area, appearing to float above the construction in the form of a pergola, link the two wings. The building shape is a cube that opens up towards the Danube and the landscape.

The architects feel that in order for the hotel to be successful and appeal to its guests, it cannot rely on a minimalist interior or exterior, or on simple technical functionality. The building applies a pronounced aesthetic which has had a magical, theatrical effect on this scenic area.

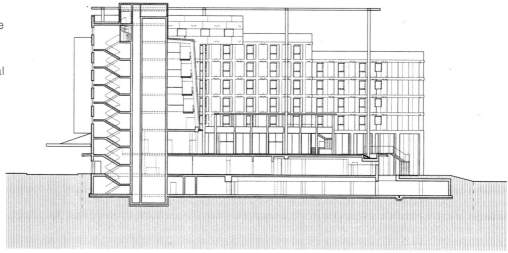

CENTRE AND BELOW: Cross-section; north elevation

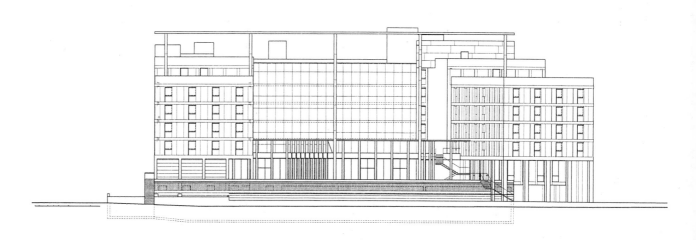

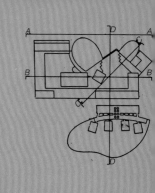

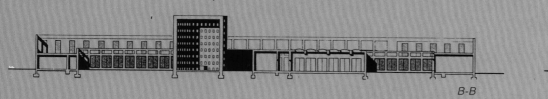

B-B

C-

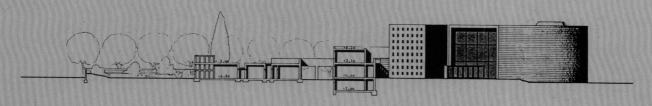

D-D

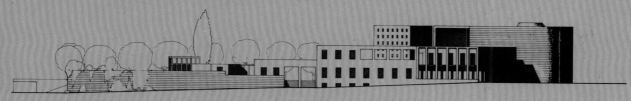

E-E

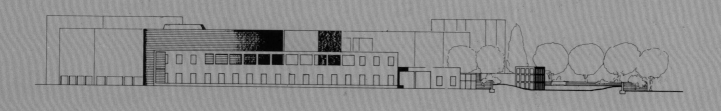

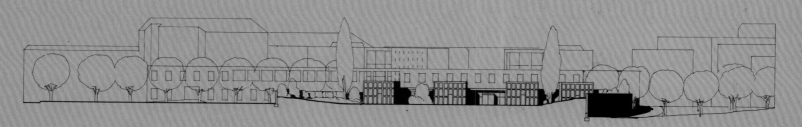

MARKET CENTRE
Bonn, Germany

Laurids and Manfred Ortner developed the concept for this urban ensemble which was completed in 1993. It is their largest project to date, and their objective was to create a central market area with community facilities, at the end of the main shopping street, Borsigallee, on Brüser Berg (Brüser Hill) in Bonn.

The Protestant community hall on the eastern side and the Catholic church to the south of the market each have high, ellipsoidal outer walls of 12 metres in height which form a gateway between the two buildings. This gateway leads from the market, up some steps and into an intimate plaza, providing access to the Protestant community hall and the Catholic church.

Both main churches are shining entities that are completely enclosed to the outside of the complex but present an open glazed facade towards the courtyard. A two-storey construction housing several community facilities surrounds the churches like a frame.

The community facilities also include a *Werketags* (Workday) church with a bell-tower, a community centre, a youth centre, a kindergarten, meeting halls, a library, an office for Catholic priests, and a Protestant parish building.

The small, casually placed pavilions are surrounded by trees, forming a self-sufficient island, with the bell-tower rising up from the centre. A south-facing kindergarten, which is housed in a pavilion, sits apart from the other buildings.

The diversity of the sculptural buildings is reflected in their form, colour and material. They form a spectacular urban group: the individual entities relate to one another significantly and form a cohesive whole. The design for the Brüser Berg urban area has effected a positive change to the entire surrounding area.

RIGHT: Site plan; OPPOSITE FROM ABOVE: Site plan; north-west elevation; section B-B; section C-C; section D-D; section E-E; elevation from the Fahrenheitstrasse; elevation from Brüser Damm

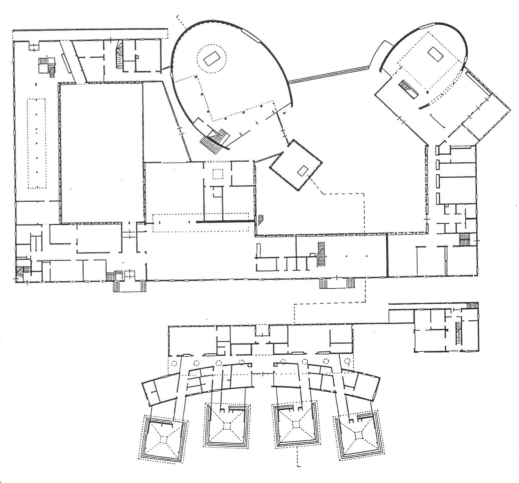

EUROPÄ DESIGN DEPOT
Klagenfurt, Germany

The Europä Design Depot has adopted an obvious and new title, the Blue Box. This indigo blue box appears to float above a sea of white pebbles. Light shines beneath the box from all sides. In the evening it is a shining cushion, made of glowing light; illuminated white blocks appear to support the 12-metre high box 60 centimetres off the ground.

Using the technology of television, the colour of the Blue Box can be replaced by a background or any chosen image. People who enter the box can later find themselves in the Colosseum in Rome or Park Avenue, New York. All types of object and environmental design can be realised with the use of this blue 'television background'. Even after the building's completion the creative design process is still part of the building.

After crossing the 'runway' through the large loading door into the interior of the box, a radically different atmosphere can be encountered. This principle of variety echoes the multiple aims of the design institution that occupies the space.

BELOW L TO R: Cross-section; longitudinal section

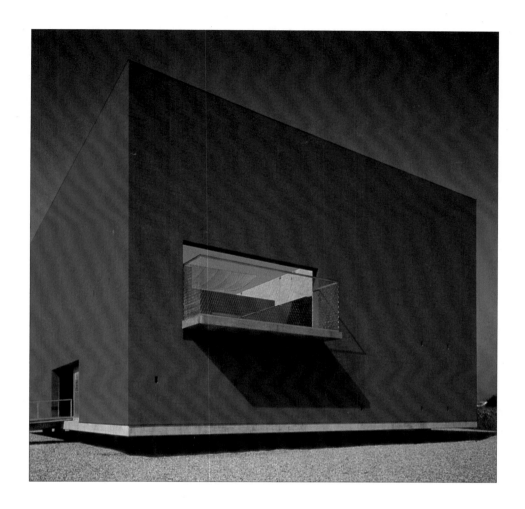

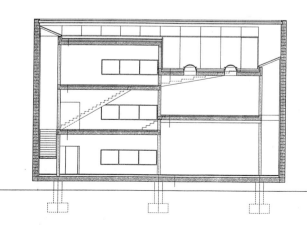
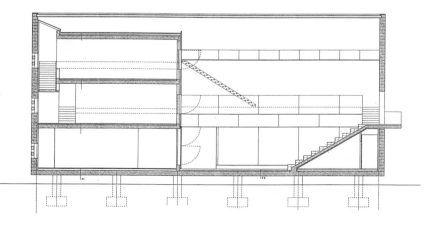

ANTOINE PREDOCK

MUSEUM OF SCIENCE AND INDUSTRY
Tampa, Florida

The spherical Omnimax Theatre becomes the key organising element of the entire facility and of the site. Contained in the museum is a lobby, major exhibit spaces, the Omnimax Theatre, education spaces, offices, and support spaces. Piers stretch to an existing facility and to the wetlands to the south creating an anchor for the site, unifying the assemblage of new and existing.

Visitors to the museum, travelling from heavily trafficked Fowler Avenue, are first struck by a shimmering, blue sphere – the new landmark/billboard for the Museum. The entry onto the site is marked by the glowing glass beacon (also doubling as a vertical circulation ramp) which guides the visitor under the building, allowing glimpses into the four-storey lobby and exhibit spaces. This drive follows the outstretched arm of the wetlands causeway, until it penetrates the thick wall and the woodlands beyond are revealed. Once parked and out of their automobile, the visitors are gathered along the edges of the 'Florida biomes' footpath, the first exhibit. This path becomes an experiential journey through several Florida biomes, from the low marshlands to the higher and drier live oak hummock at the Museum's front door.

A series of truncated 'legs' that define an outdoor adventure courtyard penetrates the building and leads the visitor into the lobby. The dining room, museum store, and library are all accessed from the entry at no charge. Views of the blue dome through the lobby to the west, and the reappearance of piers, lead the visitor beyond and into the four-storey lobby where the nested levels of exhibits seen earlier from the cars are once again visible. These overlapping levels allow exhibits to flow easily up through the facility where access is gained to the Omnimax Theatre.

Antoine Predock Architects worked in association with Robbins, Bell, Kuehelm Architects, and completed the Museum in 1995.

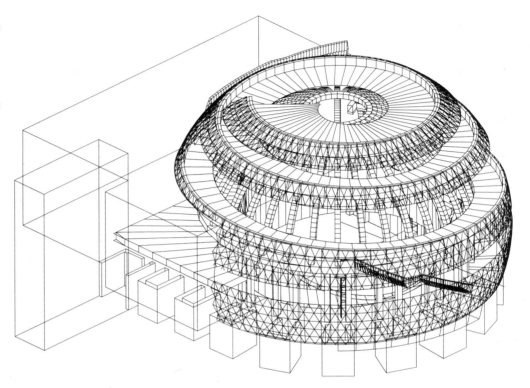

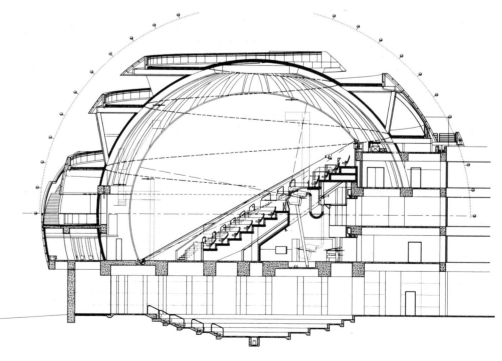

FROM ABOVE: Axonometric; section of Omnimax Theatre

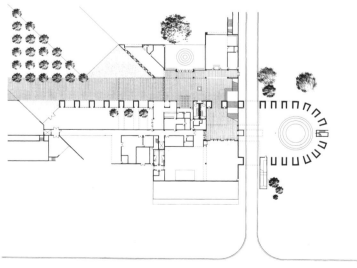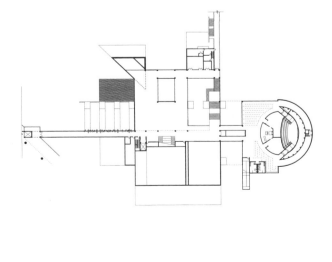

Ground floor plan; second floor plan

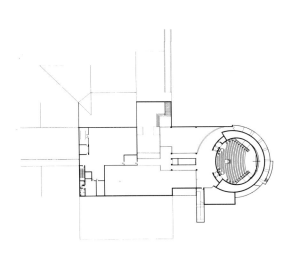

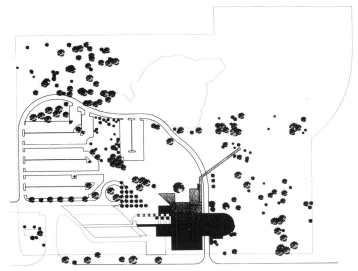

Fourth floor plan; site plan

JOHN OUTRAM ASSOCIATES

THE JUDGE INSTITUTE
Cambridge University

John Outram Associates has created over the last 20 years, together with a few regular subcontractors, a new palette of internal and external finishes that they call, generically, 'video-masonry'. They combine visual invention with the solidity of stone, and use a computerised video screen to compose colour and pattern.

All original examples of architecture began by being strongly patterned and coloured. The Parthenon was painted all over. The glint of its white marble was of no visual consequence. Never has it been more incorrectly understood than in Le Corbusier's *Vers une Architecture*. It is a sign of conceptual flaccidity to relapse into the use of 'natural materials' for surface decoration, and a sign of vulgarity to slab buildings over with exotic and expensive materials for their own sake. Outram prefers to use synthetic materials that are only stained with colour so that we can see their material substance: 'We never use entropic grey or bloodless beige unless we wish to represent death. This we do with plain Portland cement, which is, literally, ash. We prefer to create neutral effects in the way of an Impressionist painter, by combining many "taches" of pure colour. Grey is better mixed in the head than in the pot. Plain grey paint is a medium that interposes itself between a material that wishes to hide itself and a mind that wishes to disguise its thoughts. We tend to avoid solid, thick, paint except when the cash runs out and we are back in "Sheetrock City", or if we are deliberately creating a positive illusion.'

John Outram has little sympathy for most architects who complain about the state of the environment: 'Modern architecture is a part of it and is both cause and effect of the current state of our cities. I have even less sympathy for architects whose work tries to monumentalise the poetic of the decolonised shantytown, continuously shredded and patched-up to feed the tax revenues of states that do nothing of permanent value for the lifespace of their citizens.' If the environment is to achieve a radical improvement then a new architectural solution is required. Slowly, over the last 40 years, Outram has rejected open plans, heroic structures, 'natural materials', the 'service core', glass walls and undecorated surfaces. In place of this he has invented an architecture of brutal directness and monkish simplicity that performs all the tasks envisaged by the pioneers of Modernism.

The basic idea is to create a 'virtual' architecture which dissolves its material fabric into ideas. This was also the aim of Dada and of Willy Doesburg and all those brilliant bohemians who tried to clown their way towards a radical new direction. The technique is to construct a trabeated structure of generous columns and beams. These define the rooms of the building with as much sophistication or simplicity as the situation either demands or allows. All of the machinery or services needed to make the rooms work are placed inside the hollow interior of the columns and beams. False ceilings are avoided, as are false floors. According to Outram: 'They [false ceilings and floors] are odious things that destroy all solidity, permanence and thermal and acoustic comfort. To talk of function as a determinant of architectural form is to live in the stone age. Function today is mediated by machines. Rooms function in direct ratio to the money spent on finishing, furnishing and servicing them. What remains is just useful and well-ordered space, mediated by generous, solid and rational architectural members.'

The final process is the decoration of these members and the six planes that they frame: ceiling (the most important), floor (the next most important), and the four horizontal 'windows'. Colour and pattern are the media to hand. Their function is to aid the dematerialisation of this full, solid and orderly architecture. Outram feels that: 'The method of preference is to invest the decoration with a significance that feeds on the architectural member until it is consumed by a vast fabric of meaning, that slowly knits about it like the coils of a great serpent. Meaning is the midwife that sloughs off the skin of matter that has choked the city of the present day in universal illiteracy and chaotic mechanism. We cannot hope to replicate nature. Plans for "fully responsive", vitalistic structures, are as ethically dubious as they are technically naive. But we can hope to understand her. The way to bridge the gulf between technology and nature is to project this understanding into our lifespace. That way, we not only make the world we build our own, but we make it the means to become "at home" (even if only as well-meaning aliens) in the world that we do not build, the world of nature.'

The key, or lexicon, to the meanings that Outram uses is basically architectural. However, he avoids the mistake of early Modernism, which was to reject tradition and, especially, to seek to intellectualise the gross materiality of building without incorporating a phenomenology of embodiment. He finds a correspondence, like a genetic code, that links the extreme past to a view of the future. He realises this with techniques that seek to be original, 'because to copy is to kill'. In this way Outram tries to bring the past and the future to life in the present, dominating the gross materiality of existence and giving us the intellectual confidence to act boldly.

The Judge Institute is an example of these meanings – the white spirals on the cylindrical blue beams represent the idea that a rafter is literally a raft that flies, or floats, across a firmament that is as blue as the sea or sky and foams with the spiral motions of liquids and gases. The spiral also describes the icon of serpentine motion, or literally a serpent itself, which has always been the figure of the outer limits, or boundary, whether of chaos or infinity. Outram calls this technique 'Doodlecrete' because any inscription

can now be inlaid permanently into the synthetic masonry.

Their ends are plugged by another material – 'Blitzcrete' a concrete made from crushed brick, that Outram invented in 1982, for the Villa Rausing at Wadhurst. 'The Blitzcrete "plugs" recall the Latin "trabes", meaning power, by depicting the cores of the blue rafters as made of fire, with its red and yellow sparks and dying embers dancing like motes against a ground of glittering white sand.'

Outram calls the blue rafters 'logs', both because they look like the logs from which a raft is lashed together, and because they resemble the scrolls of text that derive their form from the physical unrolling of papyrus stems. This 'nest' of 'canonic' reeds surfs through the ether, carrying what Corbusier called the 'Sol Artificiel'. 'The final level is that of the 600mm (two foot) diameter, polyester coated aluminium gutter. Its *cyma recta* shape is that of the typical *corona* or *geison*. Martianus Capella, writing in AD3, described the *kyma* as the hollow metal spheres that enclose creation. The *kymata* are the waves that one finds far from the seashore when the sea bed has fallen far out of sight and everything has become mobile and fluid. The wave form of our *cyma-recta* moulding is coloured the deep blue of outer space and its fixing bolts are exaggerated in size to the glitter with a stainless brilliance, like stars.'

When John Outram Associates write their performance specifications, included is the iconography of their design. They do this so that the contractor clearly understands that any alternative, that he is at liberty to suggest, has to perform at a level of meaning as well as matter. The contractor can grasp the pictorial logic of these ideas.

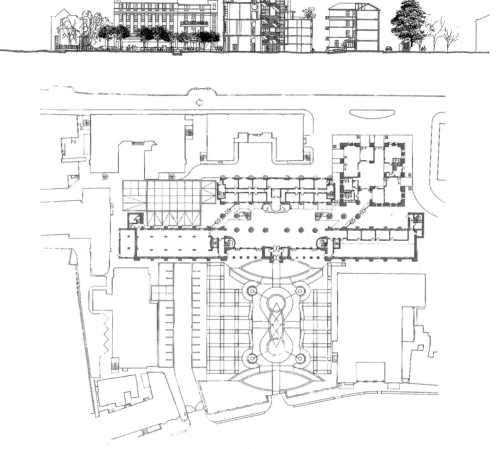

East to west section; ground floor plan

BRIAN CLARKE
HAUS DER ENERGIE
Kassel, Germany

The Haus der Energie is the new headquarters of the energy generating company Energie-Aktiengessellschaft Mitteldeutschland, in Kassel, the city famous for the 'Dokumenta' art show. This building incorporates a Brian Clarke artwork along the whole of the north facing wall. Split into two levels, the upper area, a restaurant catering to the daily needs of 500 employees, is host to a highly coloured and exuberant construction of huge amorphic forms.

The central area of each doorway was left clear and transparent by the artist. This allows the retention of substantial ambient white light in the space whilst providing an element of privacy. Also, the relationship between the internal space, the external gardens and the major autoroute into the city is harmoniously married. When interviewed about this extraordinary space the office staff from the company expressed great enthusiam for the 'optimism' it created.

Clarke's first proposal of the connected entrance hall, which is a huge and light filled three-storey space, was designed with substantial colour. Through a series of carefully orchestrated stages he finally settled on a proposal for the removal of the field of colour in favour of white opalescent glass, like milky water. Though transparent, this material acts like a gentle filter of gossamer. The central areas are again left clear, creating the impression of a series of arcades echoing directly the opposite wall of the entrance hall. In this part of the composition Clarke's ability to link internal architectural space with external natural space is at its zenith, and the subtle interplay of colours and transparent tones makes this area one of the most remarkable in the recent history of art in architecture.

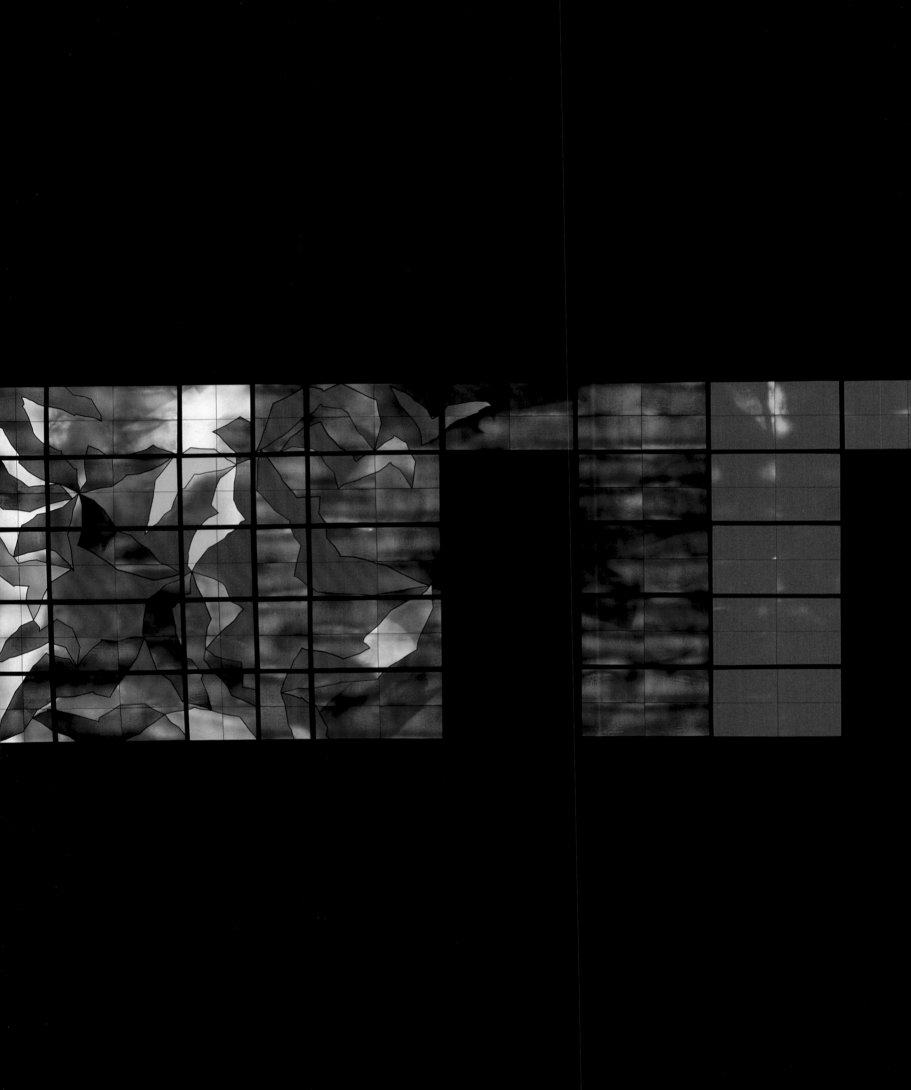

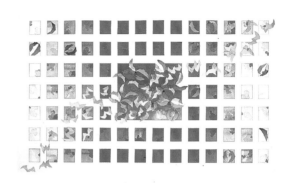

FRANKFURTER ALLEE PLAZA
Berlin, Germany

Brian Clarke designed this model of a
1,000 square metre stained glass roof
over a refurbished city block in former
East Berlin.

The project uses large areas of white
opalescent glass allowing a considerable
amount of clean light into the space and
avoids a dark gloominess in the plaza.
The coloured areas, which are predomi-
nantly cobalt blue, are interspersed and
overlaid by a diagonal movement characteristic of Clarke's amorphic elements in
deep oranges, reds and greens.

Certain motifs have preoccupied
Clarke for long periods, but given that he
has worked solely within the self-imposed
constraints of a purely abstract vocabu-
lary, the diversity of his visual forms is
remarkable. While making a series of
collages in New York he attempted to tear
out cross shapes free-hand. Intrigued by
the resulting vegetal forms, he developed
them into organic elements which he calls
'amorphs', and which he uses to subvert
the formal grid structure or repeated
geometrical symbols of his paintings.

The amorphs have figured dramatically
in several of his large-scale works in
other media. They have now become
increasingly dominant, and their affinities
are perhaps more accurately described
as biological or cartographic, rather than
vegetal.

The amorphic design on the plaza roof
is made from transparent glass allowing
carefully selected shapes of coloured
light to be projected, by direct sunshine,
onto the white internal walls of the plaza.

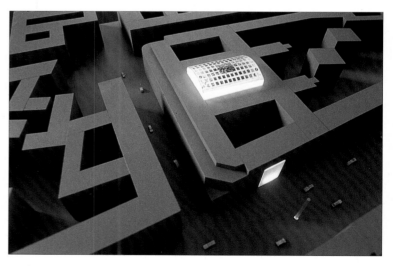

*FROM ABOVE: Rooflight design; model of
interior; site model*

CROSSRAIL STATION
Paddington, London

This 140-metre long stained glass light beam was designed for the architectural firm, Alsop and Störmer for the CrossRail Station at Paddington. The function of the glass light beam is to take natural and coloured light down onto the station platforms for the new rail link.

Brian Clarke describes William Alsop's architecture as 'all theatre and loud music – the grandeur only gradually emerges from the clamour'. Alsop says of Clarke, 'he understands the building process, he's architecturally minded. We wanted an art work which was part of the architecture but not dictated by it.'

The CrossRail Station at Paddington is designed as a deep slit in the ground, marking the route of the new line, extending alongside the existing main-line station. Viewed from below it is a railway cathedral; indeed, the height of the space from platforms to street equals that of Cologne Cathedral.

The glass 'box' was designed in a close collaboration between Clarke and the architects. There was an obvious need to retain large areas of clear glass. In fact, the balance between plain and coloured glass is very carefully considered. Clarke describes the overall composition as 'episodic'.

A particular emphasis was placed on the junction with Chilworth Street and Eastbourne Terrace, where the walker or driver faces a huge area of colour. 'It's a project to be experienced in many ways,' says Alsop, 'coming up the escalators, going down, looking up from the platform level.' From high above, the station will read as an illuminated slash of colour. Any fears about the conservatism of stained glass married with the expressive dynamism of the architecture are met with the idea that colour provides intensity that can only be achieved with stained glass.

FROM ABOVE: Model viewed from Eastbourne Terrace; front view; aerial perspective

CZWG ARCHITECTS
WESTBOURNE GROVE PUBLIC LAVATORIES
London

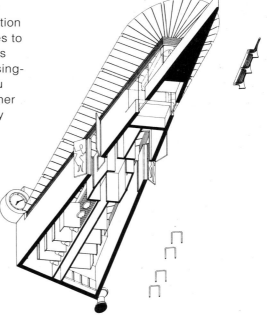

After 20 years of practice CZWG was finally commissioned to design their first public building, albeit a public lavatory.

In the early 1980s, the Royal Borough of Kensington and Chelsea filled in the underground lavatory at Westbourne Grove and erected a temporary arrangement. When ten years later the borough published plans for its permanent replacement and associated landscaping, the Pembridge Residents' Association took exception to the mediocrity of the design and commissioned CZWG to propose an alternative for a lavatory and landscaping within the council's budget. After many vicissitudes and strong pressure from the association, the council's various committees accepted the alternative and it was built and completed in July 1993.

By rearranging the inefficient car parking layout an entirely new triangular island was formed. Trees, cycle stands and specially designed benches donated by the association were arranged on plain paving with granite curbs.

The new lavatory building stands toward the south-west corner of the island. The turquoise glazed brick walls are parallel to the curb edges so forming a triangle. The projecting canopy roof is rectangular with a fan-shaped end. This geometry allows the central gutter to fall toward the wide end, while the internal spaces take advantage of the natural light through the translucent covering. The sharp end of the triangle is a glazed brick plinth which is partially enclosed with plate glass to form a flower kiosk, an idea added to the brief by the residents. The large clock on the south-west corner was also given by the association.

Dancing silhouettes on the steel entrance doors advertise the building's use when the doors are open and celebrate the yearly passing carnival.

There is something bohemian about Westbourne Grove. Turquoise seemed suitable for this rather raffish area of London, to go with the white stucco of the surrounding buildings and fit in with the trees and florists. CZWG first got the overall design through the planning committee and then hit them with the colour. The chief planning officer calmly decreed, 'well we have gone this far, let us have the architect's complete idea'. Now the locals direct people to the loo's new address as Turquoise Island.

Public lavatories tend to be anonymous and/or underground, but the notion of having extravagant public lavatories to celebrate some sort of civic pride gets half the population saying to the Kensington and Chelsea council, 'why did you spend so much money?', while the other half say, 'why do you not do this every time?'.

RIGHT: Isometric BELOW: Site plan

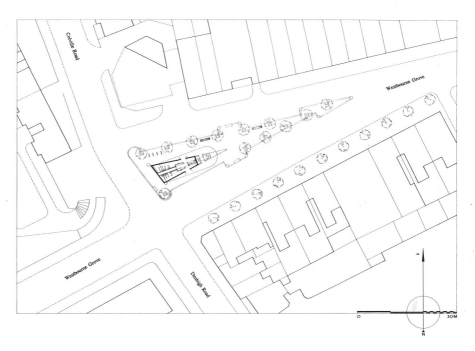

FRANK O GEHRY

VITRA INTERNATIONAL HEADQUARTERS
Basel, Switzerland

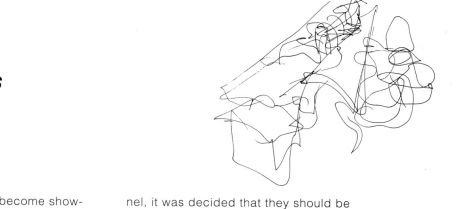

This project is a master-planned development with the first phase being a 62,000 square foot corporate office building. It is on a suburban site in Birsfelden, outside Basel, bounded by the low-rise Vitra manufacturing building on one side, and a small converted office structure on the other. The surrounding neighbourhood contains a mixture of light manufacturing, offices, houses and garden apartments. To the east is a dense forest reserve, visually tied to, but physically severed from, the site by an autobahn submerged well below grade. The existing zoning required a building of less than ten metres in height. Parking was required at a rate of one car for every three employees on site, including existing uses.

Programmatically, the building is to house various working groups which require 'changeable' office planning in a way which will allow them to demonstrate and experiment with their own furniture

lines. The offices also become showrooms, so a relatively neutral space was designed for the programme element. Much research was done to investigate the state-of-the-art office space before the project began. As a result, 'combi office' and 'office landscape' types will be accommodated as well as more traditional closed and open offices. The strict energy codes of Switzerland do not allow air-conditioning in offices, so natural ventilation is accommodated by windows and the entirely shaded south wall under a large wing-shaped canopy.

In addition to the office block, there are more 'permanent' communal support areas such as the main entrance/reception, cafeteria, switchboard, mail, meeting and conference rooms. Since these spaces were thought of as less changeable and are used by all departments of the company, including off-site person-

nel, it was decided that they should be located centrally and allow for future expansion of offices around them. The nature of these spaces also allowed them to take on richer, sculpted shapes. The size and proportion of this element is similar to the scale of some of the existing homes nearby; it thus became dubbed 'the villa'. The wing canopy houses a 'living room' atrium and formally mediates between the simple office block and the central, energetic villa.

Architecturally, the building responds to the varied scale and conditions of its context. It welcomes visitors and workers alike and provides a strong, unique image for the company within its own workspace/showroom. The structure of the building is concrete and masonry. The external materials are a combination of painted stucco, zinc metal panels, and wood-framed doors and operable windows.

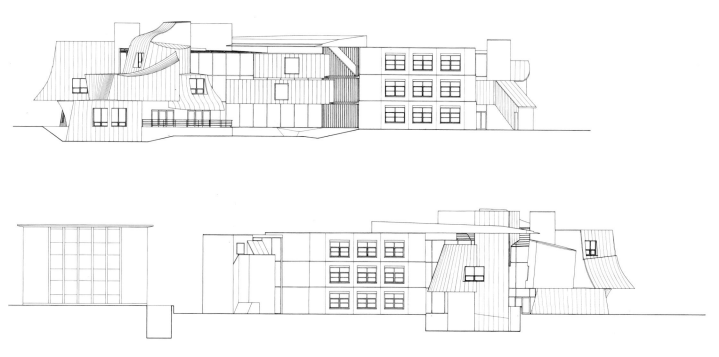

FROM ABOVE: Concept drawing by Frank O Gehry; east elevation; west elevation

85

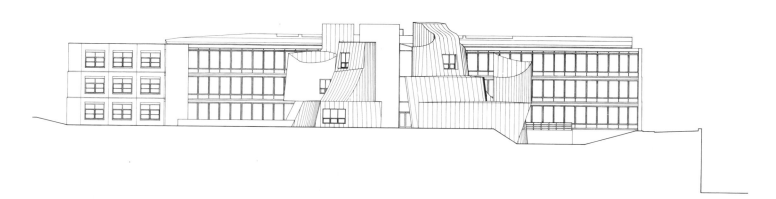

South elevation

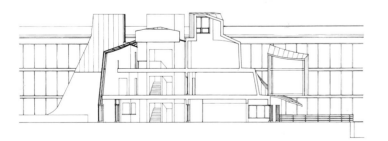

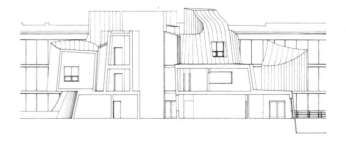

Cross-sections

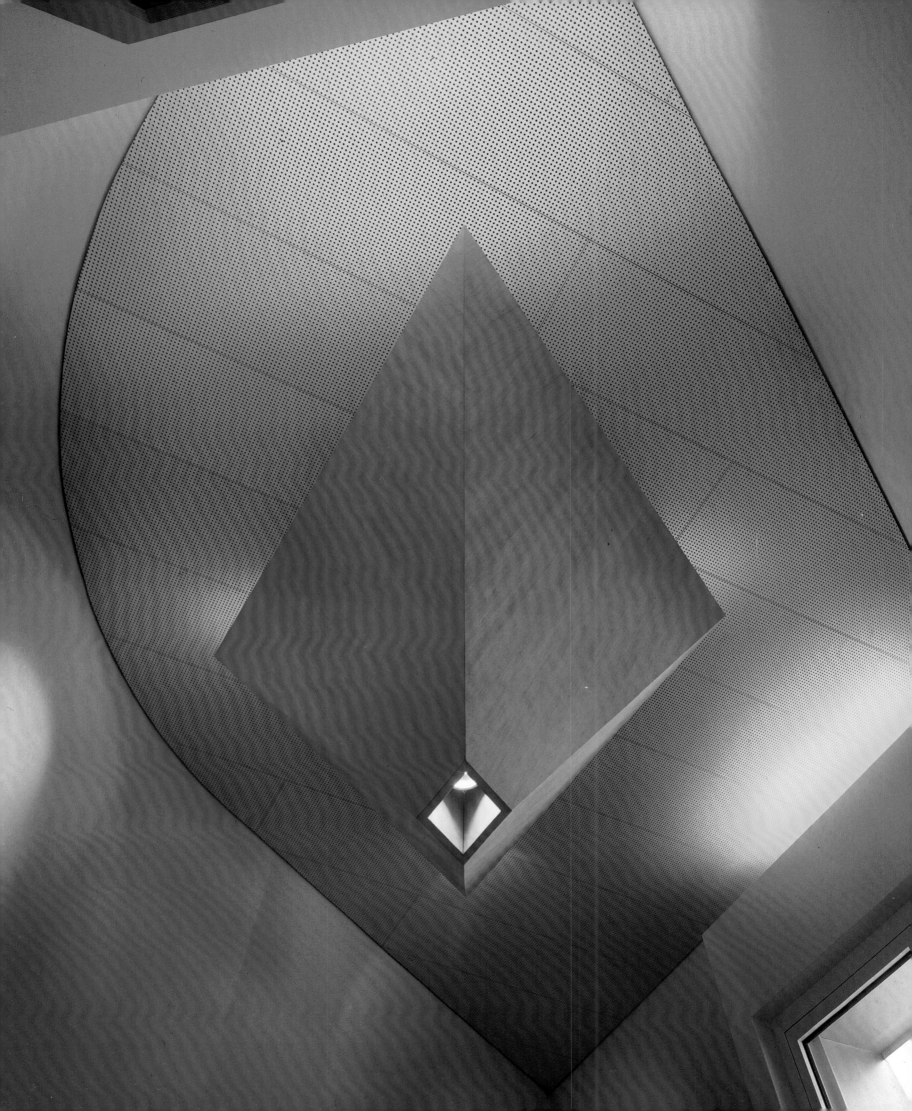

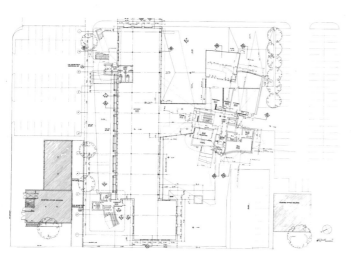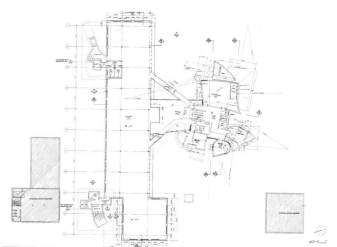

Ground floor plan; first floor plan

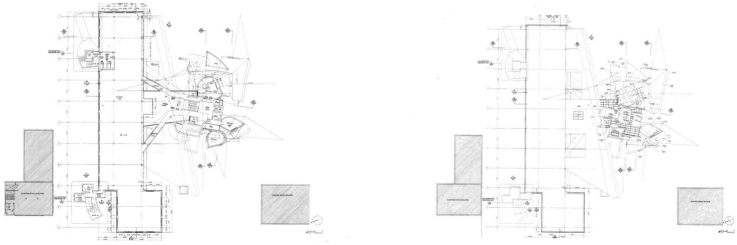

Second floor plan; roof plan

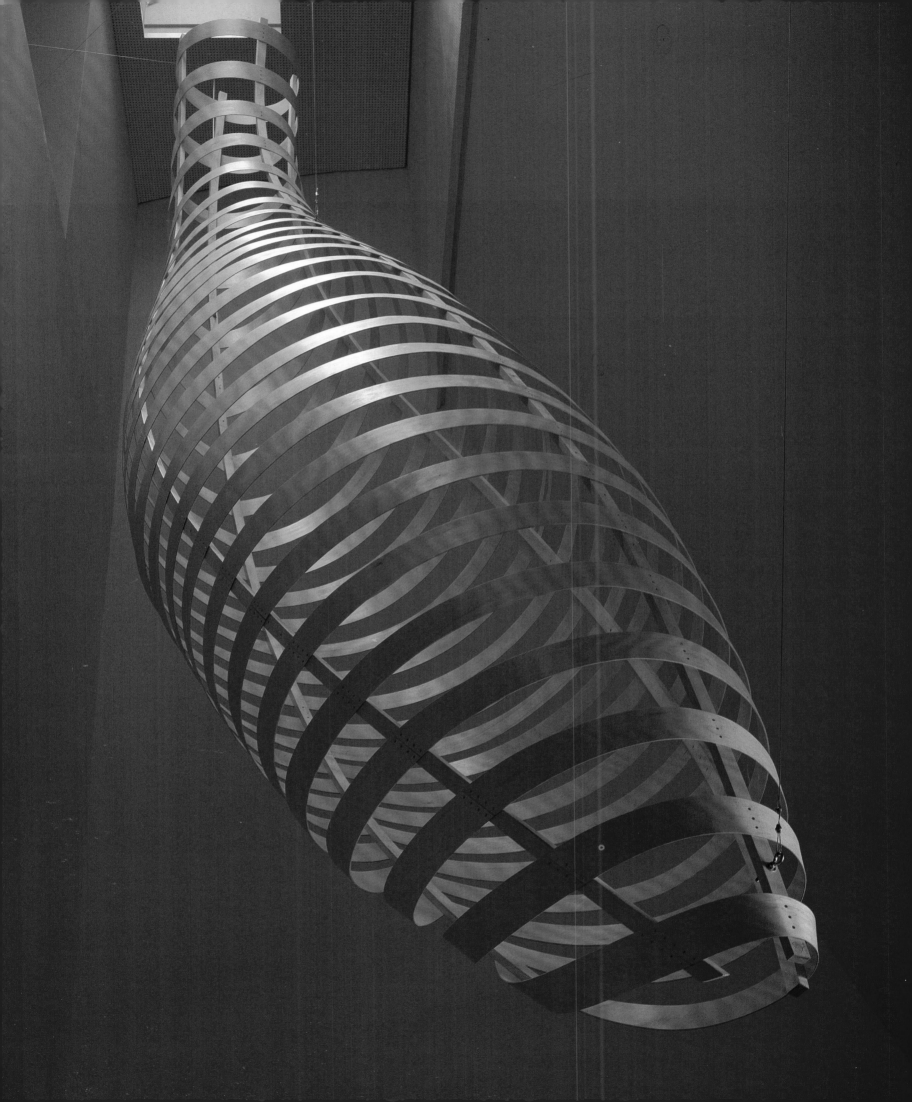

MADIGAN + DONALD
CAMDEN TICKET SHOP
London

Firstly, nothing physical or material can be bought or sold from this 'shop' which meant the architects had to plan beyond conventional retail design. Essentially the ticket shop functions as a virtual retail facility and therefore has relatively unusual security requirements – there is no actual stock and money held on the premises. As a consequence of these factors, the project was designed and detailed to express a concept of 'simulation'. A colour laminated suspended ceiling was integral to provide an enhanced definition of the host space, whilst the use of 'wood effect' laminated wall cladding panels express and represent notions of simulation.

The Camden Ticket Shop comprises of an extended sales bench, window and glass shop front. The bench takes on the form of a sculptural object which also conceals storage cabinets. The bench is constructed of timber and plywood, is finished in colour laminates and lit by concealed light fittings.

The existing window to the rear of the space was re-glazed in yellow cathedral glass ensuring constant sunshine or around the clock 'glazed prozac', and again reinforcing the concept of simulation.

Overall the use of coloured materials in this project, either as pragmatic surface protection or expressions of the architectural programme always relies on interconnecting relationships with light (either natural or electric) in order to communicate the architect's intentions. Madigan + Donald, however, was more preoccupied with the deployment of colouring agents and their physical and material characteristics than the selection of particular tones or hues which became, to an extent, a secondary consideration.

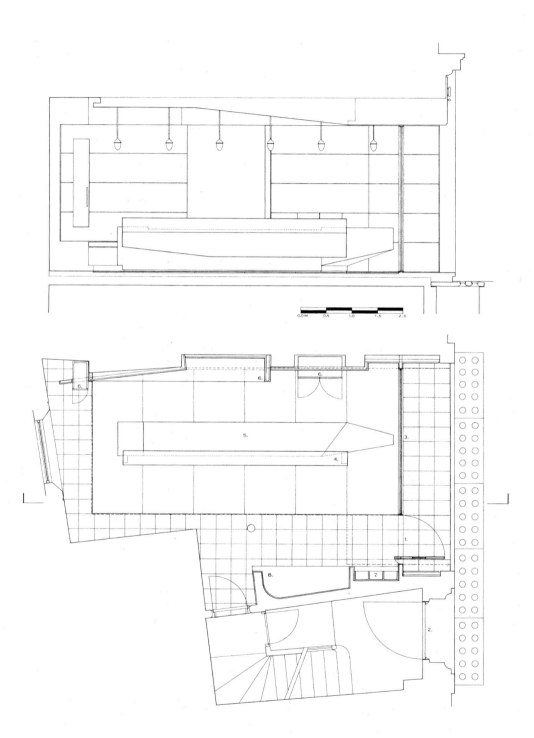

Cross-section and floor plan

I use colour, but I do not think about it while I am still at the design stage . . . What this means is that I go to the place over and over again and at different times of the day and begin imagining colours ranging from the craziest to the most incredible ones . . . Later, I ask the master-painter to paint the colour on large pieces of cardboard and to attach these to the uncoloured wall. I leave these cardboards hanging for several days, move them around, change the contrasts on the walls until I finally come to a decision.

Luis Barragán, *The New Private Realm*, Berlage Cahiers 3, p116

Images are of Colourspace, an inflatable structure of 68 ovoid units, made of vibrantly coloured PVC sheeting, created by the artist Maurice Agis.